# Evangelicalism and the Orthodox Church

A Report by the Evangelical Alliance
Commission on Unity and Truth among
Evangelicals (ACUTE)

acute

First published in 2001 by Acute

07 06 05 04 03 02 01   7 6 5 4 3 2 1

Acute is an imprint of Paternoster Publishing,
P.O. Box 300, Carlisle, Cumbria, CA3 0QS, U.K.
and Paternoster Publishing USA P.O. Box 1047, Waynesboro,
GA 30830–2047
www.paternoster-publishing.com

**British Library Cataloguing in Publication Data**
A catalogue record for this book is available from the British Library.

ISBN 0–95329–924–4

Cover Design by Campsie
Typeset by Textype Typesetters, Cambridge
Printed in Great Britain by Cox & Wyman Ltd, Reading, Berks

# Contents

# Note on Referencing

Biblical quotations are from the New International Version.

Quotations from patristic writings are taken from the *Ante-Nicene Christian Library* or the *Library of Nicene and Post-Nicene Fathers* unless otherwise stated; these editions are readily available in print, on CD-Rom and on the Internet (www.ccel.org).

A glossary of technical terms appears at the back of this report. Terms appearing in the glossary are marked with an asterisk ★ at their first occurrence.

# Preface

The following report is the result of a study on Evangelicalism and Eastern Orthodoxy by a working group of ACUTE – the Alliance Commission on Unity and Truth among Evangelicals. ACUTE was established by the Evangelical Alliance in 1995 to work for consensus on theological issues that test evangelical unity, and to provide, on behalf of evangelicals, a co-ordinated theological response to matters of wider public debate. As well as Evangelical Alliance members, ACUTE's Steering Group includes representatives of the British Evangelical Council and the Evangelical Movement of Wales.

These conversations were not 'official'; members of the group participated because of their interest in this subject and as individuals rather than delegates of any particular body or institution. The chapters of this report began life as papers presented by individuals to the group, but each member is happy to own the report in general terms.

This is not the first time that evangelicals and Orthodox in the United Kingdom have met together for discussion: in the early 1980s, a Russian Orthodox delegation headed by Metropolitan Anthony Bloom met with leaders from the Evangelical Alliance to discuss areas of common ground and share testimonies. However, no report was published.

In the late 1990s, it became evident that fresh contact needed to be made between evangelicals and Orthodox in the United

Kingdom. ACUTE agreed to sponsor a working group, and in February 1999 it was assembled. We met on six occasions up to March 2000, and produced a draft report which was circulated for peer review. The following people kindly assisted us in this way: Prof William Abraham (Perkins School of Theology, Southern Methodist University, Dallas, Texas); Rev Dr Emil Bartos (Emmanuel University, Oradea, Romania); Prof Ion Bria (Geneva, Switzerland); Prof Gerald Bray (Beeson Divinity School, Samford University, Birmingham, Alabama); Rev David Carter (Secretary, Theology and Unity Group, Churches Together in England); Mrs Kathy Carter (formerly of Keston College, Kent); Nicholas Chapman (Orthodox Christian Book Service, Staffordshire); Rev Stanley Davies (Global Connections, London); Stephen Dray (Moorlands Bible College, Sopley, Hampshire); Dr Mark Elliott (Director, Global Center, Beeson Divinity School, Samford University, Birmingham, Alabama); Dr Don Fairbairn (Erskine Theological Seminary, Due West, South Carolina; Donetsk Christian University, Ukraine); Fr Thomas Hardy (Orthodox priest, Oxford); Fr Michael Harper (Orthodox priest, Cambridge; International Charismatic Consultation on World Evangelization); John Hosier (New Frontiers International, Hove); Prof Tony Lane (London Bible College); Mgr Kevin McDonald (Oscott College, Sutton Coldfield); Rev Ken Morey (Evangelical missionary, Romania); Dr Bradley Nassif (Society for the Study of Eastern Orthodoxy and Evangelicalism; formerly of Fuller Seminary, California); Rev Theodor Oprenov (General Secretary, Baptist Union of Bulgaria); Victor Petrenko (Evangelical Pastor, Latvia; PhD Student, Durham); Dr Marcus Plested (Institute for Orthodox Christian Studies, Cambridge); Rev Dr Edmund Rybarczyk (Assemblies of God minister, California); Prof Ioan Sauca (Ecumenical Institute, Bossey, Switzerland); Rev Bill Snelson (General Secretary, Churches Together in England); Rev Dr Chris Sugden (Oxford Centre for Mission Studies); Dr Philip Walters (Keston Institute, Oxford). They read the report and their comments proved most helpful in the refining of the text, but it should not be assumed that they agree with all its findings. We also wish to express our thanks to many others who readily responded to our questions on specific issues.

We should also like to commend Miss Carolyn Skinner for the ever-efficient administrative support she provided to us. Finally, we would like to express our gratitude to Mark Finnie and his colleagues at Paternoster Press for their assistance in what has been an exciting and challenging process of theological and pastoral reflection.

## The Working Group

**Dr Tim Grass** (Editor and Working Group Convenor)

**Rev Dr David Hilborn** (Theological Advisor, Evangelical Alliance)

**Prof John Briggs** (Pro-Vice-Chancellor and Principal, University of Birmingham Westhill; member of World Council of Churches Orthodox-Evangelical consultations)

**Rev Dr Kevin Ellis** (Anglican curate, Gloucester; formerly Secretary, Tyndale Fellowship for Biblical and Theological Research)

**Fr John Jillions** (Principal, Institute for Orthodox Christian Studies, Cambridge)

**Rev Dr Nick Needham** (Lecturer in Church History, Highland Theological College, Dingwall)

**Mr Nigel Pocock** (Lecturer in Biblical Studies, Glory House, London)

**Prof Andrew Walker** (Professor of Theology, Religion and Culture, Kings College, London; Diocesan Missioner for the Russian Orthodox Diocese of Sourozh)

**Prof David Wright** (Professor of Patristic and Reformed Christianity, University of Edinburgh)

# Foreword

It is a great pleasure for me to be able to commend this excellent and comprehensive study of the links between British Evangelicalism and the Eastern Orthodox Churches represented in the United Kingdom. On the surface, it would seem that no two groups of Christians could be further apart. For example, evangelicals sit light to tradition, and worship with great stylistic freedom, whereas the Orthodox glory in their ancient liturgies. Evanglicals do all they can to make the Gospel comprehensible in modern street language, whereas the Orthodox usually worship in an ancient tongue, and even when they adapt themselves to English, it is the language of the Authorized Version which they prefer!

But as this study makes clear, evangelicals and the Orthodox hold the great fundamental truths of our faith in common. We have both done battle in modern times against the forces of unbelief, and we have both paid a high price for our faithfulness to the Gospel. More than most, we both know what it means to be pilgrims and strangers on earth, looking for a heavenly city whose builder and maker is God. Because of this, there is a spiritual sympathy between evangelicals and Orthodox which transcends all the differences of style and culture, and which has long manifested itself in small but fruitful ways. In the nineteenth century, British evangelicals, working through the Bible Society and the YMCA, did much to stimulate a similar awakening in Orthodox countries, and the heritage of patristic thought, so central to Orthodoxy, is now being increasingly widely appreciated in evangelical circles. Evanglicals may find the forms of Orthodox mysticism strange, but we have no problem with the notion that Christianity is essentially a spiritual experience of the living God, and this helps them to see divine grace at work in the most unuusal of circumstances.

Both Orthodox and evangelicals can transcend their theologies without abandoning them, because both believe that love is the fulfilment of the law, and that our God is above and beyond any of the boxes we may create for him. Furthermore, because Evangelicalism is a spiritual movement, not a church, it is not perceived by the Orthodox as a threat in the same way that Roman Catholicism. Conversely, evangelicals do not regard the Orthodox church as a spiritual dictatorship, and are therefore much more open to it than they are to Rome. The two traditions are not about to merge – history and a host of theological differences stand in the way of that. But the very fact that we are strangers to one another has its own appeal – after all, opposites attract!

It is my prayer that God will use this book to help us to grow in understanding of, and sympathy for, one another, and that as we read it, we may all draw closer to God our Saviour, for in drawing closer to him, so we will draw closer to each other and be more firmly rooted in the One in whom we live and move and have our being.

Gerald Bray
Professor of Anglican Technology
Beeson Divinity School, Samford University,
Birmingham, Alabama, USA

# Introduction

At first sight, it might be wondered why ACUTE should publish a report on Evangelicalism and the Orthodox Church in the United Kingdom. Many would be of the opinion that there are more pressing issues within British Evangelicalism which deserve prior consideration. Yet the subject may be more relevant than it initially appears, for several reasons:

1. Since the late 1980s, it has become much easier for churches in the United Kingdom to make contact with churches and other agencies in Eastern Europe where Orthodoxy is the dominant form of Christianity, and to send workers into this area. Many Western evangelical churches support missionaries or charity workers who have sought to respond to the new opportunities for proclaiming and demonstrating the love of Christ. Regrettably, the massive influx of such personnel has led to tensions and misunderstandings between ventures originating in the West and local churches and agencies, both evangelical and Orthodox. There is now a growing recognition in some circles of the need for improved co-operation, which in turn depends on a greater degree of mutual under-standing.[1]

2. There are over two hundred Orthodox congregations in the United Kingdom, with an estimated three hundred thousand

members, perhaps half a million or more if those who are nominally Orthodox are all included. They represent churches with roots in Cyprus, Greece (the vast majority), Russia (the most open to ecumenical contact), the Middle East, Byelorussia, Ukraine, Yugoslavia, Romania and Bulgaria. The United Kingdom is also home to a large community of Oriental Orthodox (see Ch. 2) from the Armenian, Coptic, Ethiopian, Syrian and Syrian-Indian Churches. While immigrant culture continues to play a formidable role in many of these communities, more and more children and grandchildren of immigrants now feel equally at home in the United Kingdom, and many will marry outside their ethnic and church community. The isolation of these communities is thus giving way to increasing engagement with life and thought in the United Kingdom. Thus evangelicals are more likely to come into contact with Orthodox believers. Bodies such as the Fellowship of St Alban and St Sergius exist to facilitate contact between Orthodox and those from other Christian traditions.[2]

3. For many years there have been conversions from Orthodoxy to Evangelicalism, perhaps more so in the Orthodox heartlands of Eastern Europe and the Eastern Mediterranean, but also in the West. With the growing Orthodox presence in the West, the number of conversions in the other direction is rising: an increasing number of people with no 'Eastern' background at all have chosen to join the Orthodox Churches, especially in the United States. Among them are a considerable number of evangelicals, some quite well known within the evangelical community.

4. As part of the rapid trend towards diversification within their constituency, evangelicals have begun to explore other traditions of spirituality and worship.[3] There is thus a value in outlining something of the ethos of Orthodoxy, a form of Christian faith which can no longer be considered as the preserve of particular ethnic groups. Similarly, Orthodox may find helpful the outline of the ethos of Evangelicalism which is provided here. We believe that contact between these two traditions presents an opportunity for mutual enrichment.

In this connection, we also note the increasing interest among British Protestants[4] and Roman Catholics in the saints of the first millennium who lived in these islands, a phenomenon connected with the growing appreciation of aspects of Celtic spirituality.[5] The significance of this is that Orthodox claim these saints as part of their heritage – because they lived before the split between East and West – and as historical precedent for the belief that Orthodoxy can flourish within a British context.

5. In recent decades, a number of dialogues or conversations have taken place between Protestants and Orthodox. At an international level, Anglicans (who are often much closer to Orthodoxy than are other Protestants), Lutherans, Reformed and even Pentecostals have begun such contact. Proceedings from some of these conversations are listed in the Bibliography. Of particular interest is the series of Orthodox-evangelical consultations sponsored by the World Council of Churches; these were instigated by the Oxford Centre for Mission Studies and the International Fellowship of Evangelical Mission Theologians. However, no such conversation has taken place in the United Kingdom – or, indeed, between any national evangelical body anywhere in the world and a local Orthodox jurisdiction.[6] Thus these conversations seek to break fresh ground, aware both of the 'global' issues affecting evangelical-Orthodox relations and of the need to earth our deliberations in a particular context.

The report is intended for an Orthodox as well as an evangelical readership. It includes Orthodox assessment of Evangelicalism as well as evangelical assessment of Orthodoxy. Both constituencies have played a part in compiling it, and we are aware that in some quarters in the West there is a fair degree of Orthodox interest in Evangelicalism. We have therefore tried to ensure that relevant aspects of evangelical thought and practice are explained for the benefit of others, in the same way that we have sought to explain Orthodox thought and practice to evangelicals. The report is not simply an assessment of Orthodoxy from an evangelical perspective, but an attempt to facilitate mutual understanding. Part I provides an overview of the issues pertinent to contact between the two traditions, out of which a number of specific topics emerge as significant; these are examined in more detail in Part II, as the basis for our conclusions and recommendations.

In recent years, there has been a renewed stress on the importance of honesty in religious dialogue. Our different beliefs are deeply held and deeply felt, and we dare not cover them over if we truly wish to build better relationships. It is vital, therefore, that neither side 'pulls its punches' when speaking about areas of disagreement. At the same time, relationships can be strengthened, perhaps unexpectedly, by a genuine appreciation of those things which we share in common and those aspects of each other's traditions which have spoken to our hearts. We trust that such a spirit is evident in this report and will be engendered by it, for there is much which we can learn from one another.

Limitations of space mean that this report cannot claim to be exhaustive; there are many avenues which we would have liked to explore further, and we hope that this may be possible in a future dialogue. In particular, deeper exploration of the philosophical and cultural frameworks within which Evangelicalism and Orthodoxy have developed, and of the exegetical foundations for their respective understandings of the Christian faith, is needed.

Readers are requested to bear in mind that this report has been produced within a context in which friendly contact and co-operation between Christian churches and groups of differing persuasions is the norm: all forms of Western Christianity have been influenced to a greater or lesser extent by the tendency to disengage religious allegiance from national identity (with the consequent rise of religious pluralism). We are well aware that the report would have been very different in tone as well as content if it had emanated from Eastern Europe. Indeed, it is questionable whether such a report could have been produced at all in that setting. Therefore great caution should be exercised in applying our judgements and conclusions to such a context. Furthermore, we note that within the Western setting there are differences between British and American manifestations of Evangelicalism and Orthodoxy; some of these are more significant than others, but to take account of them would have lengthened and complicated the report unduly. Thus we emphasize that the report reflects the specific context within which it was produced.

We are conscious that some of what follows demands sustained concentration, although suggestions for further reading include a number of introductory works to which readers may wish to turn. However, we hope that the report will serve to introduce readers to some of the issues which are most pertinent to the development of evangelical-Orthodox relationships, and in so doing promote a greater understanding of one another's traditions which will enrich the body of Christ.

## Notes

1 A valuable resource exploring theological, cultural and practical issues relating to ministry in Eastern Europe is the *East-West Christian Ministry Report*, produced by the Global Center, Beeson Divinity School, Samford University, 800 Lakeshore Drive, Birmingham, AL 35229, USA. Web site: {www.samford.edu/groups/global/ewcmreport/}

2 Fellowship of St Alban and St Sergius, 1 Canterbury Road, Oxford, OX2 6XH; e-mail: gensec@sobornost.org. The Fellowship produces a journal, *Sobornost*.

3 The increasing diversity within Evangelicalism is explored by James Davison Hunter, *American Evangelicalism: Conservative Religion and the Quandary of Modernity* (New Brunswick, NJ: Rutgers University Press, 1983); the same author's *Evangelicalism: the Coming Generation* (Chicago, IL: University of Chicago Press, 1987); David Wells, *No Place for Truth: or, Whatever Happened to Evangelical Theology?* (Grand Rapids, MI: Eerdmans, 1993).

4 Although the practice of referring to 'Protestants and Anglicans' has become increasingly widespread in ecumenical circles, Anglicans have been treated as Protestants for the purposes of this report; those of evangelical convictions would consider that this is where they belong.

5 Contemporary interest in Celtic spirituality is evident throughout much of British Christianity. It seeks to adopt and adapt aspects of the prayer life of Celtic forms of Christianity as they developed during earlier centuries. In the United Kingdom, most inspiration is drawn from the Scottish

strands of the Celtic tradition. The resulting reconstructions vary widely in content and faithfulness to the sources: some could best be classified as 'New Age', others have been strongly shaped by wider ecumenical and social concerns, still others would doubtless be recognized easily by Celtic saints. See D. E. Meek, *The Quest for Celtic Christianity* (Edinburgh: Handsel Press, 2000).

6 The history of Orthodox-evangelical discussion is outlined by Bradley Nassif in 'Eastern Orthodoxy and Evangelicalism: The Status of an Emerging Global Dialogue', *Scottish Bulletin of Evangelical Theology* 18.1 (Spring 2000), pp.21–55. Dr Nassif is the secretary of the Society for the Study of Eastern Orthodoxy and Evangelicalism, whose annual theological conferences in the United States feature leading Orthodox and evangelical speakers. For further details, contact him at 88 Tierra Montanosa, Rancho Santa Margarita, CA 92688, USA; e-mail: blnassif@yahoo.com.

# 1

# What is an Evangelical Christian?

There are several ways in which we may answer the question, 'What is an evangelical?' Here we offer an answer which combines historical, doctrinal and experiential definitions.

## i) Historical: the term 'evangelical' in church history

Many who call themselves 'evangelical' would emphasize the roots of the term in the New Testament word *euangelion* ('the good news'): evangelicals see themselves as people with good news for the world. Thus, in describing themselves as evangelicals, they are not merely claiming descent from ancestors such as John Wesley (1703–91), his brother Charles (1707–88) and George Whitefield (1714-70), but making a claim to stand in the essential tradition of New Testament Christianity. Indeed, many would say that the evangelicals' answer to the question 'What is an evangelical?' represents nothing other than their answer to the question 'What is a Christian?'

Historically speaking, apart from occasional uses prior to the Protestant Reformation (the Oxford theologian and philosopher John Wyclif (c. 1330–84) was known as *doctor evangelicus*, 'the evangelical doctor'), the term 'evangelical' achieved prominence as a description of those who held to the teaching of Martin Luther (1483–1546) concerning justification by faith alone. It then came to be used of the Reformed as well as the Lutheran communities; in

Germany, for example, *evangelisch* is widely used as equivalent to 'Protestant'.

Evangelicals have often emphasized their debt to the Reformers, the Puritans★ and the Pietists★, and there is a high degree of continuity between these movements and Evangelicalism. However, the most influential contemporary definition of what it means to be an evangelical, put forward by the historian David Bebbington, sees it as referring to a movement which emerged during the eighteenth century. He sees four features as continuing characteristics of the movement – *conversionism, activism, biblicism* and *crucicentrism*.[1] Another writer explains these as:

> ... conversionism (involving a call to personal repentance and moral transformation): crucicentrism (evangelicals have centred their theology on the cross of Christ, the doctrine of the Atonement being central to their theological understanding); biblicism (the Bible being taken as the supreme authority in matters of faith and practice); and activism (a commitment to doing which springs from the moral radicalism rooted in a sense of personal responsibility).[2]

While little of the theology of the eighteenth-century evangelicals was new, they tended to apply it rather differently from their immediate forebears.[3] In particular, many in England stressed that assurance of salvation was the normative pattern of Christian experience (as had the sixteenth-century Reformers) and that this could be given to an individual in a moment – in contrast to the frequent seventeenth-century Puritan emphasis on the need for lengthy (often lifelong) preparation for grace, and the resulting uncertainty regarding one's true spiritual standing and struggle for assurance of salvation. Such assurance gave evangelicals the freedom and the inner dynamic for their famed activism in preaching the gospel and engaging in good works.

From the beginning, there was a plurality of strands within English-speaking Evangelicalism, most evident in the divergent courses taken by the Wesleys and Whitefield. The former espoused a robustly Arminian theology, while the latter unashamedly proclaimed Calvinist doctrine; yet both saw themselves as faithful to the *Thirty-Nine Articles* of the Church of England. As well as doctrinal plurality, there was plurality in churchmanship: in the

United Kingdom, for example, there were evangelicals with roots in the historic nonconformist denominations (Baptists, Independents or Congregationalists, and Presbyterians), evangelicals who were committed members of the established churches, such as the Church of England or the Church of Scotland, and (from the nineteenth century) evangelicals who belonged to one of the various newly founded denominations or non-denominational faith communities. To some extent, this plurality was the result of a tendency which was evident in Pietism to downplay the significance of doctrinal and ecclesiastical differences in favour of an emphasis on shared experience; this was seen as a means to realizing greater unity among believers.

Nowadays, evangelical plurality is strikingly evident in the problematic issue of how, or even whether, evangelicals and fundamentalists are to be distinguished.[4] 'Fundamentalism' is a term used by the media to refer to any type of dogmatic (and often backward-looking) thought, usually in religion. However, it came to prominence as a description of the theology of a series of papers, *The Fundamentals*, published in America from 1910 in an attempt to uphold and strengthen Evangelicalism's hold on its traditional beliefs. After the Second World War, a division between evangelicals and fundamentalists became evident in North America over the legitimacy and extent of Christian social involvement and co-operation with non-evangelicals. More recently, disagreement has focused on such matters as the state of Israel and its role in Biblical prophecy, involvement in (and relationships with) 'mixed' denominations, the role of scholarship and reason in Christian thought, and biblical inspiration and interpretation. Considerable tension has sometimes resulted. These differences are evident not only in traditionally Protestant nations, but also in the divergent attitudes of evangelicals and fundamentalists towards non-Protestant Christianity, especially in Orthodox Europe.

## ii) Doctrinal: evangelical belief

Doctrinal definitions often concentrate on evangelical distinctives at the expense of those truths which evangelicals hold in common with non-evangelicals. Yet what is important to evangelicals is not necessarily distinctively evangelical. Consider, for example, their Christology. Karl Barth, an evangelical in the Continental rather than the English sense, provides a helpful definition of evangelical theology:

> The qualifying attribute 'evangelical' recalls both the New Testament and at the same time the Reformation of the sixteenth century. Therefore, it may be taken as a dual affirmation: the theology considered here is the one which . . . first achieved unambiguous expression in the writings of the New Testament evangelists, apostles and prophets; it is also, moreover, the theology newly discovered and accepted by the Reformation of the sixteenth century. . . . What the word 'evangelical' will objectively designate is that theology which treats of the *God of the Gospel*. 'Evangelical' signifies the 'catholic', ecumenical (not to say 'conciliar') *continuity and unity* of this theology.[5]

On many fundamental doctrines, such as the Trinity or the incarnation, the Reformers would have been in broad agreement with Catholic (and Orthodox) theologians: all would have appealed to the definitions put forth by the same councils of the early church (see the Appendix). Indeed, evangelicals have often seen themselves simply as the purest expression of mainstream catholic Christianity. However, Reformation thought is often seen as marked by the following four theological distinctives:

- *Scripture alone:* Scripture alone possesses supreme authority. All other authorities, such as the Fathers, church councils or the papacy, were regarded as subject to criticism and correction in the light of Scripture.
- *Faith alone:* believers are justified (declared righteous before God) not on the grounds of anything they have done, but as they place their faith in the atoning work of Christ on the cross and are thus united with him.
- *Grace alone:* salvation is a gift of God and his initiative is primary. It owes nothing to human works or achievements. Even the believer's exercise of faith in Christ is itself the effect of God's grace at work in the heart, rather than an independent response originating with the human will.

- *Christ alone:* there is only one mediator between humanity and God – Jesus Christ. Thus the Reformers rejected any idea of saints as mediators, and rejected an ecclesiastical system which emphasized priestly mediation of divine grace to the faithful through the sacraments.

Some evangelicals consciously seek to uphold these Reformation distinctives and emphasize what they see as the confession-based nature of historic Evangelicalism.

Today, Evangelicalism's defining beliefs could be summarized as follows:[6]

- The supreme authority and entire trustworthiness of Scripture as the word of God.
- The restoration of a relationship with God broken through sin as humanity's deepest need.
- The sufficiency of Christ as the only mediator between humanity and God (which entails belief in the incarnation).
- The substitutionary nature of Christ's atoning death (historically, not all evangelicals have held this view of the atonement, but it is affirmed in the Doctrinal Basis of the Evangelical Alliance).
- The insistence on salvation as entirely the gracious gift of God.
- Justification, the declaration by God that believers are accepted as righteous, as an act of his grace, received through faith in Christ.
- Christianity conceived in terms of a personal relationship with God which provides the context for a growth in holiness made possible by the indwelling of the Holy Spirit.
- The expectation of the personal and visible return of Christ.

Orthodox will note with concern the absence of reference to the Church from either of the above lists.

It is important to reiterate that evangelical theology at its best has sought to be not so much self-consciously distinctive from other traditions as faithful to the Scriptures, the revealed and sufficient word of God. The concept of 'evangelical theology' thus refers to method as much as to conclusions, a method which is governed by the question: 'What do the Scriptures say?' Such an emphasis helps evangelicals to live with a diversity of opinions on a range of theological issues which are not perceived as threatening the fundamentals of Christian faith, since they can justify widely differing views on baptism, for example, as equally motivated by concern to be faithful to the teaching of Scripture. All the same, such diversity often confuses outside observers, and leads some (including Orthodox) to conclude that Evangelicalism does not possess a coherent doctrinal tradition. It is only as we combine doctrinal and experiential perspectives that the picture becomes somewhat clearer.

### iii) Experiential: evangelical understandings of the spiritual life

What makes evangelicals perceive themselves as such? Is it the doctrines they believe, the church to which they belong, the style of worship they prefer, or the approach to mission which they practise? All these (and more) go to make up the evangelical self-portrait (though the resulting images do not always look too similar), but more significant than any of these is the dimension of spiritual experience, of which Ephesians 2:1–10 may serve as a summary statement. Alan Gibson, former secretary of the British Evangelical Council, has defined an evangelical as 'someone who has heard, believed and received the authentic good news of Christ in genuine experience, . . . it expresses **what they are** before it says anything about **what they understand**'.[7] Evangelicals have insisted that this experience is one of personal trust in Christ as expressed in repentance for sin and faith in the efficacy of his work on the cross, and generally they have said that this – apart from any sacramental act – is what makes a person a Christian (see Ch. 10 for the outworking of this in personal spirituality). Thus it has been asserted that Evangelicalism is 'as much a devotional ethos as it is a theological system . . . Christian orthodoxy, as set out in the ecumenical creeds, with a particular emphasis upon the need for the personal assimilation and appropriation of faith'.[8]

This emphasis on the primacy of personal faith in Christ means that evangelicals have usually felt that they had more in common with evangelicals in other denominations than with non-evangelical fellow-denominationalists. They have tended to see themselves as part of a fellowship, stretching across denominational boundaries and bound together by a common experience of conversion rather than by a shared theological tradition – although they would share belief in the basic tenets listed above. They have been described as a constituency rather than a church or confession, although the primary meaning of 'church' for evangelicals has been the local congregation rather than any formally constituted denominational body (see Ch. 7). While Evangelicalism has this ecumenical impulse at its core, it differs both from the institutionalized ecumenism of the World Council of Churches and the conciliar ecumenism of Orthodoxy in that it is based on a bond which is invisible.

Evangelical spirituality is not simply a matter of personal faith; considerable attention is also given to the biblical teaching regarding the 'new birth' (Jn. 3:1–8; Jas. 1:18; 1 Pet. 1:23). Evangelicals affirm that becoming a Christian involves divine as well as human action: in the new birth (or 'regeneration') the Holy Spirit makes alive those who formerly were spiritually dead (Eph. 2:1,5). A number of the sixteenth-century Reformers saw this as happening at baptism in the case of the elect (those chosen by God to be saved), but this view is now rare among evangelicals in the United Kingdom.

Moreover, the Spirit who gives life to those who were dead continues to be active in believers, making them aware of their standing as children of God (Rom. 8:14-17; Gal. 4:6), transforming them into the likeness of Christ (2 Cor. 3:18; cf. Gal. 5:22-3) and gifting them for service within the body of Christ (1 Cor. 12:7).

## iv) Conclusion

The experience of the gospel has been the primary driving force for evangelicals: having been grasped by it, they seek to proclaim it through word and deed. They see a personal relationship with Christ as necessary to salvation; furthermore, they see the proclamation of this to all (even those nominally Christian) as the heart of the 'Great Commission' (Mt. 28:18–20).

All this explains two things. Firstly, evangelicals have been great activists, and this includes the involvement of all in proclaiming the evangel (cf. Bebbington's inclusion of activism as a hallmark of Evangelicalism). Secondly, most evangelicals have distinguished between first-order and second-order doctrinal issues, the former being directly related to our salvation and the latter being issues on which there is disagreement among the saved. Although they have often disagreed vigorously over whether particular doctrines, such as ecclesiology or the doctrine of the sacraments, should be regarded as first-order or second-order issues, the doctrine of salvation tends to take centre stage in evangelical theologizing, certainly at a popular level. Thus establishing the meaning of the term 'evangelical' matters greatly to evangelicals because it rests upon a particular understanding of what is meant by the evangel, the good news of salvation through Christ.

An adequate definition of what it means to be an evangelical must take account of *all* the aspects of Christian faith and life covered above. The following definition attempts to do so and is offered as a summary of the perspective from which this report has been produced:

> *An evangelical is a Christian who lives under the authority of Scripture in all matters of belief and practice and who experiences a personal relationship with Christ founded on repentance and faith. Such a person will accept the fundamental doctrines affirmed by the ancient Creeds, and regard the history of the evangelical tradition as their history.*

## Notes

1 D. W. Bebbington, *Evangelicalism in Modern Britain* (London: Unwin Hyman, 1989), p. 3.

2 D. M. Lewis (ed.), *The Blackwell Dictionary of Evangelical Biography* (Oxford: Blackwell, 1995), vol. I, p. xix.

3 In parts of Eastern Europe, evangelicals who owe their immediate origins to movements of the eighteenth rather than the sixteenth century are often known as 'Neo-Protestants'.

4 The most recent investigation of this issue is Harriet A. Harris, *Fundamentalism and Evangelicals* (Oxford: Oxford University Press, 1998).

5 Karl Barth, *Evangelical Theology* (London and Glasgow: Fontana, 1963), p. 11.

6 For further discussion of evangelical theological convictions, see the ACUTE Report, *What is an Evangelical?* (obtainable from the Evangelical Alliance).

7 Alan Gibson, 'Contemporary Trends in Evangelicalism', *Foundations* 33 (Autumn 1994), p. 2.

8 Alister McGrath, *Evangelicalism and the Future of Christanity* (London: Hodder & Stoughton, 1993), pp. 52–3.

# 2

# What is Orthodox Christianity?

Orthodoxy is a family of self-governing churches united by a common faith, a common liturgical order (see Ch. 9) and a common church order. The common faith is expressed in the Creed of Nicea-Constantinople (also known as the Nicene Creed) and the doctrinal decisions of the first seven Ecumenical Councils (for which see the Appendix). Orthodoxy has no counterpart to the Pope, as there is equality among the leaders of its various national churches (jurisdictions), although the Ecumenical Patriarch, based in Constantinople, now Istanbul in Turkey, is accorded a primacy of honour.

The Eastern church has experienced several significant divisions. Two of these resulted in the formation of churches which are known today as 'Oriental Orthodox'. The first and larger group, including the Syrians, Copts, Armenians and Ethiopians, are those who refused to accept the Chalcedonian Definition of 451; they were formerly known as 'Monophysites' from their insistence that the incarnate Christ was one nature, not two. Recent scholarship has concluded that the divisions between them and the Chalcedonian Orthodox churches are less significant than had been thought, and signs of convergence are now evident between them and mainstream Orthodoxy. Although they have communities of adherents in the United Kingdom, they do not play a significant role here in the theological or ecumenical spheres, and the focus in this report is primarily on Chalcedonian (or 'Byzantine')

Orthodoxy. The second group, the 'Church of the East' found mainly in Iran and Iraq, were often known as Nestorians from their adherence to views condemned as those of Nestorius at Ephesus in 431: in an attempt to safeguard the doctrine of the full humanity of Christ, a clear division was made between his human and divine natures to the extent that the union between them was weakened considerably. They also questioned the practice of describing Mary as *theotokos*★, 'God-bearer', which was an expression of the belief that, from the moment of his conception, Christ was Son of God as well as Son of Man. Again, recent scholarship has questioned whether the divisions are as significant as was believed in the fifth century.[1]

However, during the medieval period a momentous division occurred in the Christian church between East and West. In 1054, the papal legate Cardinal Humbert deposited a bull of excommunication against the Patriarch of Constantinople in the church of Hagia Sophia; the Patriarch responded by anathematizing Humbert. The importance of these events was probably more symbolic than real: they confirmed a separation that had already taken place. East and West had been growing apart for hundreds of years before this: such factors as different languages (for much theological writing the East used Greek, the West Latin), different cultural and philosophical backgrounds, and the break-up of the Roman Empire (the Western Empire collapsed in the fifth century, but the Eastern Empire continued until 1453) all played a part in this process. Theological factors which precipitated the crisis included the addition in the West of the *Filioque* clause to the Nicene Creed, which declared that 'the Spirit proceeds from the Father *and from the Son*'. This was finally given papal sanction early in the eleventh century (for further details see the section on the *Filioque* dispute in Ch. 6). The East believed that only an Ecumenical Council had authority to alter the Nicene Creed (which had been issued by just such a Council), whereas the Pope's approval of the alteration implied a claim to such authority. Thus theological differences were inextricably linked with different approaches to church government.

The Western church, which was under the jurisdiction of the

Bishop of Rome, continued as what we now call the Roman Catholic Church. The division between East and West hardened with events such as the sack of Constantinople by crusading soldiers in 1204. Councils at Lyons (1274) and Ferrara/Florence (1438–45) tried to secure reconciliation, but the Orthodox found themselves unable to accept their decisions. By the Reformation era, most Western scholars knew little about the contemporary Eastern church.

Although it is true that evangelicals and Orthodox have both separated from Rome, we should beware of attaching too much significance to this in Orthodox-evangelical discussion. In many ways, Protestants and Catholics have much more in common than do Protestants and Orthodox; they both originated as Western European traditions, and the division between them came centuries after that between Rome and the East. Thus, to the Orthodox, the big difference is not that between Protestant and Catholic, but between East and West. Evangelicals will be wise, therefore, to avoid regarding Orthodoxy as 'Catholicism without a pope': the differences between the two communities are considerably deeper than such a description implies.

## i) Apostolic continuity

As might be expected, the Orthodox claim historical and theological continuity between their communion and the church of the early centuries: 'The Orthodox Church does not need to give proof of its historical authenticity; it is simply the direct continuation of the Church of the Apostolic Age.'[2]

Today, if you go to many of the places mentioned in the New Testament and look for a church, you are likely to be pointed in the direction of an Orthodox church. In all these places Orthodoxy is the native Christian tradition. The people on the street, even those who are only formally Orthodox, still have the intuition that the Orthodox have maintained unbroken the life of the apostolic church. The Orthodox Church believes itself to be 'the same in essence and spirit in the twentieth century as it has been from the beginning. The church has developed over the centuries, but it is the same church, in the same way as a grown up person corresponds to the picture taken of him as a child.'[3] Thus there is a certain inevitable exclusiveness, however politely it may be expressed, about Orthodoxy's attitude towards other Christian bodies, because the Orthodox believe that they have preserved the fullness of apostolic Christianity in a way that other churches have not.

This sense of continuity with the apostolic church which the Orthodox maintain has been central to Christian identity from the beginning, as is evident in these passages from the New Testament:

> They devoted themselves to the apostles' teaching (Acts 2:42).
> Timothy, guard what has been entrusted to your care (1 Tim. 6:20).
> Guard the good deposit that was entrusted to you (2 Tim. 1:14).

The apostles' doctrine, handed down from one generation to another in accordance with these instructions, 'would have been valueless without the miracle of Pentecost, unless the Spirit had come not merely to the Twelve but to the entire Church'.[4] The Spirit calls the Church into existence and guides her life (Jn. 16:13). Indeed,

> . . . it is the Spirit who defines the canon of Scripture in the Church and preserves the Church through the centuries in truth and faithfulness to its Head . . .

> Scripture includes the *totality* of the apostolic witness and nothing can be added by way of completing our knowledge of the person of Jesus, his work, and the salvation which he has brought us; but this written witness regarding Christ was not launched into a void − after the manner of the Koran, which, according to Islamic tradition fell from heaven and is read by men in a form fixed once and for all − but was given to a community which has been founded by these Apostles and which received the same Spirit.[5]

The Orthodox point out that the church existed prior to the New Testament. Guided by the Spirit, it was councils of the church which confirmed which books should be included in the canon of Scripture. The early church thus understood the 'deposit' to be guarded as much broader than the text itself.

This became especially clear in the Trinitarian and Christological debates of the first six centuries of Christian history, when all sides were appealing to the words of Scripture. St Basil of Caesarea (c.330–79) insisted that the full life of the church from apostolic times had to be included as evidence in the debate.

> Of the beliefs and practices whether generally accepted or publicly enjoined which are preserved in the Church some we possess derived from written teaching; others we have received delivered to us 'in a mystery' by the tradition of the apostles; and both of these in relation to true religion have the same force. And these no one will gainsay; – no one, at all events, who is even moderately versed in the institutions of the Church. For were we to attempt to reject such customs as have no written authority, on the ground that the importance they possess is small, we should unintentionally injure the Gospel in its very vitals . . .[6]

In Basil's mind, Scripture did not stand alone as the deposit of faith, but was part of the Christian tradition of those things which had been believed 'everywhere, always and by all'.[7] This phrase, from the famous 'Vincentian Canon' (after its fifth-century originator, Vincent of Lérins), expressed the view then held by the church: Scripture was the final authority, but because of the potential for diversity of interpretation it should be explained in accordance with that which had been taught throughout the Church (the criterion of universality), by those of all generations (the criterion of antiquity), and accepted by the body of the faithful (the criterion of consent). 'The criterion of universality required that a doctrine, to be recognized as the teaching of the church rather than a private theory of a man or a school, be genuinely catholic, that is, be the confession of "all the churches . . . one great horde of people from Palestine to Chalcedon with one voice re-echoing the praises of Christ".'[8]

The criteria of apostolic continuity were already clearly elaborated by the second century. According to St Irenaeus of Lyons (c. 130–c. 200), the apostolic tradition which was handed down in churches of apostolic foundation included three elements:

1. the tradition of revelation 'handed down to us in the Scriptures as the pillar and bulwark of our faith';
2. the tradition of doctrine 'derived from the apostles', summarized in a precursor of the creeds known as the 'Rule of Faith';
3. the tradition of ecclesiastical structure represented by 'those who were by the apostles instituted bishops in the churches, and . . . the succession of these men in our times'.[9]

These criteria of apostolic continuity were regarded as inter-dependent, so much so that some of the Fathers could even say that the Scriptures could only belong to those who were in the Church, who accepted these assumptions. Thus they refused to debate the Scriptures with heretics. Tertullian (c.160–c.220) justified this refusal on the ground that the heretics used (or rather misused) the Scriptures to win over the faithful. 'If in these lie their resources, before they can use them, it ought to be clearly seen to whom belongs the possession of the Scriptures, that none may be admitted to the use thereof who has no title at all to the privilege.'[10] Heretics were to be admonished, not debated with; in any case, he considered that debate never convinced a heretic but served only to unsettle the faithful. The point to consider was:

'With whom lies that very faith to which the Scriptures belong? From what and through whom, and when, and to whom, has been handed down that rule, by which men may become Christians?' For wherever it shall be manifest that the true Christian rule and faith shall be, *there* will likewise be the true Scriptures and expositions thereof, and all the Christian traditions.[11]

And that faith, for Tertullian, was to be found in the churches founded by the apostles, which were the depositories of the apostolic faith and which handed it down through the generations.

It was St Ignatius of Antioch (c.35–c.107) who was the first to refer to a threefold pattern of ministry of bishops, priests and deacons as an essential aspect of church life and organization, something which has remained fundamental to Orthodox, Catholic and Anglican ecclesiastical structures. The bishop (who at that time would rule over a local congregation rather than a larger area) was the focus of the congregation's unity, presiding over it as God's representative. He conducted baptisms, by which individuals were admitted to the fellowship, and celebrated the Eucharist, which gave visible expression to the congregation's unity as well as nourishing it with 'the medicine of immortality'.[12] The Ignatian emphasis on the bishop as the focus of unity was intended as a safeguard against the entrance of heresy: it was the bishop, as guardian of the apostolic tradition of doctrine, who was responsible for teaching the flock and who was empowered by the Spirit for that task.

Orthodoxy believes that the Church is *holy* – not just a human institution – precisely because it has always been guided by the Holy Spirit speaking through every aspect of its life: its Scriptures, councils, saints, teachers, liturgical life, iconography and so forth. This sense of being guided by the Spirit throughout history also keeps the Church from being tied to any external criterion of truth: the Church is 'the church of the living God, the pillar and foundation of the truth' (1 Tim. 3:15).

The understanding of apostolic continuity in the early church has been emphasized precisely because on the one hand this remains essential to Orthodox identity and because on the other hand it is perceived by Orthodox as a fundamental difference between themselves and evangelicals (and Protestants generally). For their part, evangelicals would wish to question whether it stands up to historical investigation; at the least, they would suggest that it needs careful qualification.

With reference to the criteria put forward by St Irenaeus which were noted above, Jaroslav Pelikan has suggested that

> . . . each of the assumptions about apostolic continuity came into question in the period of the Reformation, with the result that each of these three criteria of apostolic continuity (and all of them together as a complex of authority) faced unprecedented challenges . . . In many ways that radical break was an anticipation of the very critiques of orthodoxy and apostolic continuity that were to come from modern thought in the eighteenth, nineteenth and twentieth centuries . . .[13]

However, the mainstream Reformers all accepted the first, and (as far as the early church was concerned) the second also; it was the third which the condition of the contemporary church forced them to deny, although some were nevertheless concerned to ensure that their newly appointed bishops were provided with a pedigree of succession which did not begin afresh but could be traced back through the centuries via the very church which they had left.

### ii) 'The Church is vast'

If the Spirit preserves the Church's apostolic continuity and gives a context to interpretation of Scripture, among Orthodox he is understood to operate mysteriously everywhere in the universe. One of the most frequently used prayers in the Orthodox tradition, an invocation of the Holy Spirit, stresses this indefinable, elusive and illimitable aspect:

> O heavenly King, the Comforter, the Spirit of Truth, everywhere present and filling all things, Treasury of blessings and Giver of life, come and abide in us, and cleanse us from every impurity and save our souls, O good One.

If the sense of being in an ancient, apostolic church is vital to Orthodox identity, so is the sense of being in a church which puts the mysterious, cosmic, limitless life of the Holy Spirit at the centre of its prayer. Metropolitan Anthony Bloom, head of the Russian Orthodox Church in Britain, writes: 'The Church is vast. So vast that it holds both heaven and earth. So vast that all people of all nations, of all cultures, of all languages are its home.'[14] Similarly, Bishop Kallistos Ware says of his own early experience in the Liturgy: 'I realised that we . . . were part of a much larger whole, and that as we prayed we were being taken up into an action far greater than ourselves, into an undivided, all-embracing celebration that united time and eternity, things below with things above.'[15]

It is this divine vastness that the Orthodox sense in the Church and which makes them humble before it, slow to judge it, to change it, to accuse it, to malign it or despise it (cf. 1 Cor. 11:22). To be sure, on a human level the Orthodox Church is a religious institution riddled with plenty of sins and temptations, but beneath all this is the conviction that the Spirit preserves in it an unbroken stream of divine life. How else, through all the tragedies of church history, are we to understand the Lord's promise that 'the gates of Hades will not overcome it' (Mt. 16:18) and his assurance, 'surely I am with you always' (Mt. 28:20)?

### iii) The Orthodox Church in Britain

The Orthodox Church speaks in many accents today, often unexpected. Indeed, if people have become accustomed to thinking of the Orthodox as 'Eastern', then they may be surprised that the Orthodox themselves, especially in Britain, are very much at home with the deep *Western* roots of Orthodoxy. Although scholarly Orthodox patristic studies rarely discuss many of the Western Fathers, St Alban, St Augustine of Canterbury, St Patrick, St Columba and St Cuthbert are as much a part of the Orthodox world as any of the Russian or Greek saints.

If the Orthodox are becoming less removed from the rest of British society, they are also less removed from each other. The so-called Orthodox *diaspora* (communities and individuals with ethnic and religious roots in Orthodox lands) in the United Kingdom, Western Europe, North America and Australia are a potential breeding ground for a new spirit of inter-Orthodox unity.[16] This, and the unprecedented freedom of most Orthodox Churches to regulate their own lives, free from state control and religious oppression, can allow Orthodoxy, for the first time in centuries, to recover a sense of its universality or catholicity, and to step out of its various cultural cocoons, its centuries of isolation and persecution. All of these have been important factors in the formation of such bodies as the Institute for Orthodox Christian Studies in Cambridge, the first Orthodox theological college in this country. They have also facilitated greater Orthodox involvement in ecumenical bodies such as the British Council of Churches and its successor, Churches Together in Britain and Ireland. The Orthodox themselves are no newcomers to ecumenism (although they are deeply divided over it): in 1920 the Patriarch of Constantinople issued a far-sighted call to all Christian churches to seek greater unity.

## iv) 'Strange Orthodox Church'

Almost two centuries ago Henry Holland, a physician from London, wrote a memoir of his trip to Greece and described his impressions of the Orthodox Church in Larissa. He was taken with the dignity and simplicity of the bishop who presided at the service, but beyond that there was nothing he found inspiring. He judged it harshly as strange and superstitious.

> In the Greek worship, yet more than in the Catholic, there is an accumulation of trifling details and exterior observances . . . which often offend the judgment by their frivolity, or by their connection with the superstitions of antecedent ages . . . The Greek church, deriving its character from an age when religion was alike subservient to the ignorance of bigotry, and to the selfish purposes of a corrupt and declining monarchy, has retained its pompous minuteness of ritual, even while labouring under the evils of Turkish oppression, and when no longer able to invest with the show of grandeur the seeming puerilities of a superstitious worship.[17]

Aspects of the Orthodox Church may look just as strange today to many evangelical observers and even to some Orthodox, and many British evangelicals would probably concur with the substance, if not the harsh manner of expression, of his assessment. So much of the history of Orthodoxy has been lived in isolation from the West and from the Reformation and post-Reformation debates that spawned the evangelical tradition. So much of its history is a record of survival under persecution and oppression. But as one Orthodox writer observes, beneath this apparent strangeness one can find incomparable Christian joy.

> Strange Orthodox Church, so poor and so weak . . . maintained as if by a miracle through so many vicissitudes and struggles; Church of contrasts, so traditional yet at the same time so free, so archaic and yet so alive, so ritualistic and yet so personally mystical; Church where the Evangelical pearl of great price is preciously safeguarded – yet often beneath a layer of dust . . . Church which has so frequently proved incapable of action – yet which knows, as does no other, how to sing the joy of Pascha!*[18]

## Notes

1  For further information on these two families of churches, see David P. Teague (ed.), *Turning Over a New Leaf: Protestant Missions and the Orthodox Churches of the Middle East* (London: Interserve, 1992²).

2  Archbishop Paul of Finland, *The Faith We Hold* (Crestwood, NY: St Vladimir's Seminary Press, 1980), p. 15.

3  Ibid.

4  John Meyendorff, *The Orthodox Church: Its Past and Its Role in the World Today* (London: Darton Longman & Todd, 1982), p. 6.

5  Ibid.

6  St Basil, *On the Holy Spirit*, §66.

7  Vincent of Lérins (fifth century), *Commonitorium [Aid to Memory]* 2.3, quoted in Jaroslav Pelikan, *The Christian Tradition: A History of the Development of Doctrine* vol. 1 (Chicago: University of Chicago Press, 1971), p. 333.

8  Ibid., p. 335, citing Jerome, *Against Vigilantius,* §5. Doctrinal development was not excluded by the Vincentian canon, so long as it represented the elaboration of what was already present embryonically in the tradition. The canon has been the subject of debate among scholars of all traditions during recent decades.

9  Ibid., p. 305, citing Irenaeus, *Against Heresies*, 3.1.1, 3.2.2, 3.3.1.

10  Tertullian, *On the Prescription against Heretics*, §15.

11  Ibid. §19.

12  Ignatius, *Letter to the Ephesians*, §20.

13  Jaroslav Pelikan, *The Christian Tradition: A History of the Development of Doctrine* vol. IV (Chicago: University of Chicago Press, 1985), p. 305.

14  Quoted by Margaret Long, in T. Doulis (ed.), *Toward the Authentic Church* (Minneapolis, MN: Light & Life, 1996), p. 128.

15  Ibid., p. 146.

16  The Orthodox in the West also face serious internal disunity, evident in the continuing inability to establish one jurisdiction with responsibility for all Orthodox in the United States and in the division within Russian Orthodoxy between Moscow Patriarchate and the 'Russian Orthodox Church Abroad'; this division occurred during the early communist years but continuing disagreement over theology and attitudes to ecumenism, especially in the West, hinders attempts at reconciliation.

17 Sir Henry Holland, *Travels in the Ionian Islea, Albania, Thessaly, Macedonia . . . During the years 1812 and 1813* (London: Longman, Hurst, Rees, Orme and Brown, 1819², vol. I), pp. 392, 394.
18 Fr Lev Gillet (1893–1980), quoted in Doulis, p. 168.

# 3

# Common ground between Evangelicalism and the Orthodox Church

The common ground between Orthodoxy and Evangelicalism is largely hidden from sight. It is to be found in the invisible depths, the structural foundations of the two traditions of Christianity. If this analysis is correct, then we should together ask how we may give fuller overt expression to the significant area of common ground that superficial comparison fails to notice.

There are obvious reasons why most evangelicals and Orthodox, even in the United Kingdom, are unaware of this common ground. They have had no firsthand experience of each other's tradition. They have rarely had exposure to each other as neighbours. A wide gulf of unfamiliarity, ignorance and incomprehension yawns between the two, to an extent that does not hold for evangelicals and Roman Catholics.[1] Orthodoxy, for example, has no Pope or British cardinal whose high public profile keeps his church in the news (although in England the Orthodox Metropolitan Anthony Bloom has been well known in wider church circles for many years).

At the level of external appearances, Orthodoxy and Evangelicalism seem poles apart. Orthodoxy's elaborate, long liturgy with formalized ceremonial and colourful vesture, sometimes in an ancient language, its use of material elements such as incense, and much else make it a strange world to most evangelicals. The ethnic base of many Orthodox church communities, the mystical ethos of their spirituality and the contemplative or passive flavour of their discipleship contrast markedly with evangelical piety. When Western evangelicals encounter Orthodoxy, it often strikes them as more alien than modern Roman Catholicism. This is partly because Orthodoxy in its various churches is often defined by nationalities whose languages English-speakers rarely learn – Greek Orthodox, Russian Orthodox, Romanian Orthodox, Serbian Orthodox, Bulgarian Orthodox, and so on.

For these reasons, among others, a presentation of shared convictions and emphases will have to overcome a considerable degree of ignorance and perhaps suspicion that lack of contact has allowed to develop.

## i) Doctrinal conservatism

Both Orthodoxy and Evangelicalism are conservative in holding to the apostolic presentation of Jesus Christ and the giving of the Spirit and the birth of the Church in the New Testament. Both hold to the historicity of the apostolic record – to the virginal conception of Jesus in Mary, to his ministry and healings and other miracles, to his bodily resurrection and exaltation and awaited reappearing from heaven at the last day (1 Cor. 15:3–8; Phil. 2:6–11; 1 Tim. 3:16; Tit. 2:11–14, 3:4–7). Both adhere to the truths expressed by the credal declarations of the early church, especially by the Nicene Creed and the Chalcedonian Definition. (Orthodoxy does not accord the same significance as the West to the so-called Apostles' Creed, which does not carry the authority of an Ecumenical Council of the Church.) Evangelicals who see their doctrinal heritage as coming from the Protestant Reformers more than from later leaders often share those Reformers' high estimate of the writings of the early Fathers, insisting that these be seen not as 'Orthodox' in any partisan sense but as belonging to the whole church, East and West. Many evangelicals may be non-credal, on principle or in practice (by deliberate or unthinking non-use of creeds), but faith in the Trinity and in the deity and humanity of Christ is an essential aspect of evangelical belief (Mt. 28:18–20;

Rom. 1:1–6; 1 Cor. 12:4–6; Eph. 4:4–6).

Here again common ground is partly obscured by the less explicit or self-conscious Trinitarianism or Christological definiteness of some strands of Evangelicalism. This means that Evangelicalism cannot be regarded as a whole as espousing any one model of Trinitarian or of Christological understanding. Nevertheless, Orthodox and evangelicals are united in believing in the incarnation in line with 'the great tradition' of the church in both East and West (see Ch. 5). As for the *Filioque* clause, few evangelicals regard it as a first-order issue. This means that they are slow to empathize with the central importance of the issues which Orthodox believe are raised by its addition, such as the right to alter a universally accepted creed and the nature of authority in the Church.

## ii) Scripture

Undergirding this shared set of credal convictions is a shared high view of Scripture as inspired by God (2 Tim. 3:14–17; 2 Pet. 1:20–1; see Ch. 8). Orthodox do not think in terms of *sola Scriptura*★ (which in any case came to sharp expression in the sixteenth-century divide, in which the Eastern churches were not involved), but they regard Scripture as given by inspiration of God. The two traditions may not use the same epithets to affirm its full truthfulness and reliability, but they join in so affirming. They have different ways in worship and personal devotion of giving expression to the holiness of Scripture, but both balk at the half-truth (so dangerous when it claims to be the whole truth) that 'the Bible is just like any other ancient book'. It has an honoured place in both Orthodox and evangelical worship.

## iii) God

Both Orthodox and evangelicals confess God to be the creator and sustainer of the world. In the Greek of the Orthodox Liturgy, Christ is worshipped as *Pantokrator* ('Almighty'), which speaks precisely of his role in sustaining creation. In practice, Orthodox differ as evangelicals do on the relation between scientific and biblical-theological accounts of the origins of the earth and of humanity, but both believe in the truth of the early chapters of Genesis, rightly interpreted. The cosmos gains its life and meaning only from its divine Creator, who will one day renew it eternally in the new heavens and the new earth. The world thus depends on God for its existence, and is not self-contained or self-explanatory (Jn. 1:1–5; Acts 17:24–8; Col. 1:15–17; Heb. 11:3). Yet there is no Orthodox dogma on how the world was created, any more than consensus on the issue is a defining mark of Evangelicalism.

Nor are God's being and activity wholly confined to this world. God is related to this world and its history not only as everywhere-and-always-present (immanent) but as apart from and above it (transcendent), reigning in heaven where his will is perfectly fulfilled. Both Orthodox and evangelicals resist reductionist views of God which identify him solely and exhaustively with 'the ground of our human being', that is, the deepest dimension of this-worldly existence.

## iv) Eschatology

Evangelicals share with Orthodox, as with many other conservative Christians, faith in the visible return of Christ, 'the resurrection of the dead and the life of the world to come' (1 Cor. 15; 1 Thes. 4:13–5:11; Rev. 21). The future hope finds expression in a variety of visions and expectations in both communities, but both believe in the promise of transfiguration completed hereafter beyond death. This is a hope not merely of individual personal glory but of the end of the ages and the consummation of all things in Christ (cf. Eph. 1:3–14). Orthodoxy has a stronger sense than most evangelicals of salvation as release from bondage to decay and corruption (Rom. 8:18-25), but both communities believe in the life of the world to come as one which involves bodily resurrection. And for both communities, the reappearing of Christ as Lord and King is a fundamental belief. Orthodoxy has a strong grasp on the interconnectedness of the whole cosmos, arising from its belief in the Spirit as 'everywhere present and filling all things', and hence tends towards a more cosmic view of redemption in which the whole created order (not merely humanity) is restored to perfection. (Such a view is also becoming increasingly popular in evangelical circles.) Concerning the understanding of the biblical teaching about hell, somewhat similar tensions are discernible in Orthodoxy to those which have more recently surfaced among evangelicals.[2]

## v) The Church and its mission

Orthodoxy and evangelical Christianity both believe in the Church in a way that distinguishes them from those who focus on the wider kingdom of God or who hold inclusivist or universalizing views which devalue the Church (see Ch. 7). Evangelicalism has been notoriously weak in ecclesiology, and has generally shrunk from speaking of the Church as a divine entity. This weakness became manifest during the eighteenth century as evangelicals in different denominations sought to explain the sense of unity resulting from their shared experience of the new birth. One reason why this weakness remains today is simply that Evangelicalism has become more a movement or a constituency than a church or communion of churches. Evangelicals commonly find their focus for unity in interdenominational or nondenominational organizations and activities. Yet Evangelicalism shares with Orthodoxy the conviction that salvation is received in human experience and is inseparable from incorporation into the Christian community (Acts 2:38–42; Rom. 6:1–4; 1 Cor. 12:12–27; Eph. 2:11–22). The Church as the essential context in which the life of God in the Spirit is given to believers is in some sense a unifying bond between Orthodox and evangelicals. 'No salvation outside the Church', found in third-century Cyprian and sixteenth-century Calvin alike, may not come comfortably to evangelical lips; nevertheless the evangelical's insistence that eternal destinies are determined in this life in response to the presentation of Christ in the gospel is not far from making the Church essential in the economy* of salvation, since it is by the Church that Christ is presented.

What, then, of the missionary and evangelistic dimension of the Church's life, on which evangelicals have always been so insistent (see Ch. 11)? Indeed, evangelicals have from time to time been so immersed in para-church evangelism as to sit loose to building up the membership of the visible church. Thus the Great Commission (Mt. 28:18–20) has become separated from the Church. The Orthodox, by contrast, often appear to have placed more emphasis on maintaining a Christian civic order and culture, although they have a missionary heritage rich with inspiration for contemporary missiology.[3] For them mission has for long periods been a matter of enduring persecution and martyrdom, and they have often seen their churches as given a divine vocation to suffer. Evangelicals need to know more about the sufferings of Orthodox churches not only in the twentieth century under Stalinism and the Soviet Communist empire but also long before, under Islam in the Middle East and the Balkans. The faith has been handed on, not only in families but also by various quiet ministries which should not be dramatized by calling them 'underground'. And some Orthodox church leaderships have seized energetically the new opportunities opened up by the revolutions of 1989.

Shared concern about perceived syncretism within ecumenical circles was a factor which brought Orthodox and evangelicals closer together: though both are willing to talk with members of other faiths, neither would wish this to be taken as implying a belief that all faiths are of equal validity as ways to God, or a rejection of the necessity for mission (Jn. 14:6; Acts 4:12, 17:30–1; Rom. 1:16–17).

## vi) Christian experience

It follows from the above that there is common ground also in the Christian experience of the Spirit (see Ch. 6). Orthodoxy may envisage this more in sacramental and ecclesial terms, but they would agree with evangelicals that men and women are called to experience regeneration, rebirth into participation in the life of God himself, through the Holy Spirit. This is an anticipation of heaven itself and may be spoken of as 'a new creation' (1 Cor. 12:1–13; 2 Cor. 5:16–17; Eph. 2:4–10). Thus Orthodoxy and Evangelicalism both maintain, more strongly than most present-day historic Western church traditions, a sense of access by the Spirit into a transcendent realm of experience. This is an emphasis of Evangelicalism that is found much earlier than the charismatic renewal. Both Orthodox and evangelicals have also been readier than most other traditions to recognize the reality of miracles worked by the power of God in the ongoing experience of his people.

## vii) Ethics

Orthodox and evangelicals share considerable common ground on significant contemporary ethical issues, notably those of ecology, sexual ethics and bioethics.

Ecology has been recognized in ecumenical and ecological circles as an area in which Orthodox teaching about the universe as God's creation, coupled with its insistence that we are not redeemed *from* the created order but *with* it and as part of it (cf. Is. 65:17–25; Rom. 8:18–23),[4] has much to offer Western Christianity in its struggles to answer allegations that the Judeo-Christian tradition is to blame for the earth's ecological plight. Some evangelicals have been ready to acknowledge this.

In the realm of personal ethics, Orthodox and evangelicals share a belief in the divine ordering of marriage and the family, and concur in refusing to recognize homosexual practice as acceptable in the sight of God (Mt. 19:3–12; Rom. 1:24–7; Eph. 5:21–33). Evangelicalism has hardly ever formalized the vocation to lifelong celibacy as Orthodoxy has done, but in practice it has often recognized the sacrificial service that only single men and women could have given (cf. 1 Cor. 7:32–8). To put it another way, most evangelicals still reject the assumption of contemporary Western culture that sexual fulfilment is essential to human flourishing. Both Orthodox and evangelicals affirm the good gift of sexuality within the ordinance of marriage between man and woman, and Orthodox parish clergy (though not bishops) are usually married.

At the same time, evangelicals and Orthodox have different approaches to the task of determining how we should live. Orthodoxy is much less inclined to make ethics a distinct discipline, finding guidance not so much in ethical analysis itself as in worship and spirituality. In a collection of essays entitled *Living Orthodoxy in the Modern World*, a writer on bioethics counsels a recovery of the root Greek meaning of euthanasia ('dying well'), which contrasts with modern understandings. He underscores 'the traditional tasks Christians should undertake in dying well',[5] such as prayer, repentance and almsgiving. The integrity of the moral life is attained through deification, in the monastery rather than the academy. Evangelical ethicists, on the other hand, have not been backward in grappling with the complex technicalities of reproductive medicine among other issues, in the setting of highly professionalized debate.

## viii) Conclusion

Spelling out common ground in this manner, that is, without at the same time identifying unshared ground, may be misleading; this chapter tells only part of the story. Every square metre of common ground charted here might be mapped differently if the focus were on ground not shared in common. Nevertheless, the area of agreement is extensive and significant. Orthodox and evangelicals are committed to a Christianity that holds uncompromisingly to God's self-revelation in Israel and supremely in his incarnate Son, Jesus Christ, to which the inspired Scriptures bear wholly truthful witness. This revelation attests a divine rescue mission in which God himself came to save his own creation mired in sin and death (Eph. 2:1–18). The first fruits of this salvation become the experience of all who in this life are incorporated into Christ in the body of the Church. It will be fully realized in the renewal of creation in the life of the world to come. Evangelicals and Orthodox alike seek to confess historic, apostolic, biblical, credal Christian faith, the faith 'once for all entrusted to the saints' (Jude 3).

## Notes

1 For an attempt to remove some of the ignorance, see Mark Elliott, 'For Christian Understanding, Ignorance is Not Bliss', *East-West Church & Ministry Report*, 1 (Summer 1993), pp. 5–6.

2 For more detailed exposition of evangelical views regarding hell, see another report in this series, *The Nature of Hell* (Carlisle: Paternoster, 2000).

3 See James J. Stamoolis, *Eastern Orthodox Mission Theology Today* (Maryknoll, NY: Orbis, 1986).

4 Paulos Mar Gregorios, 'New Testament Foundations for Understanding the Creation', in Wesley Granberg-Michaelson (ed.), *Tending the Garden: Essays on the Gospel and the Earth* (Grand Rapids, MI: Eerdmans, 1987), p. 85.

5 H. Tristram Engelhardt, in Andrew Walker & Costas Carras (eds), *Living Orthodoxy in the Modern World* (London: SPCK, 1996), p. 127. Note also Kallistos Ware''s essay in this volume, 'Lent and the Consumer Society'. Engelhardt has offered an Orthodox perspective on bioethics in *The Foundations of Christian Bioethics* (Lisse, Netherlands: Swets & Zeitlinger, 2000).

# 4

# Differences between Evangelicalism and the Orthodox Church

Meetings between evangelicals and Orthodox often follow a pattern of mutual congratulation on the discovery of a convergence of interests in many areas, followed by an appendix listing matters where ongoing work needs to be done to reduce tensions. For example, the 1995 meeting in Alexandria sponsored by the World Council of Churches listed the following seven areas where further work was required:[1]

1. Divergent ecclesiologies
2. The sacraments
3. The saints and their veneration
4. The place of Mary in the faith of the Church
5. Differing baptismal theology and practice
6. Our understanding of salvation
7. Effective mechanisms for co-operation in common witness

However, this chapter proposes a slightly different agenda, under six headings, around which discussion could helpfully take place.

## i) Church and movement

Our starting point has to be the intrinsic difficulty of the exercise. It is not possible to travel far in understanding Orthodoxy without engaging with its understanding of the nature of the Church, notwithstanding the existence of a variety of canonical jurisdictions within both Eastern and Oriental Orthodoxy. By contrast, Evangelicalism characterizes a movement spread through a variety of churches, some exclusively evangelical, or nearly so, and some which are not. One could say that Orthodoxy is a church (or confession) while Evangelicalism is a constituency (or movement). This contrast points up a problem which complicates relationships between the two: The Orthodox are more used to relating to institutions and their self-understanding includes the aspect of belonging to a united and visible church tradition, whereas there is no body which can speak authoritatively for the whole of Evangelicalism.

Furthermore, because there is no one evangelical ecclesiology but rather a plethora of evangelical ecclesiologies – sometimes episcopal, sometimes presbyterian, sometimes congregational – and because of the emphasis on individual faith, some evangelicals have a very under-developed sense of the significance of the Church. This contrasts with Orthodox reverence for the Church and their reluctance to criticize it. For the Orthodox, the Church is not just a collection of believers or forgiven sinners: it is always the holy body of Christ (1 Cor. 12:13; Eph. 1:22–3), embracing a presence both on earth and in heaven, a definition from which thoughtful evangelicals would not wish to diverge.

There is here a crucial area for discussion concerning the relative importance of the individual and of the community. This will emerge, for example, in areas of missionary activity where often there is a gulf of non-understanding between individualistic, or even sectarian, para-church missionary enterprises, and the pastoral concern of a church which has many centuries of witness in a given area (see Ch. 11).

## ii) Scripture and Tradition

In comparing these two faith families with liberal Protestantism, common ground of respect for the biblical revelation quickly appears. But it is not long before the implications of the previous point begin to emerge: evangelical championing of freedom for each individual to engage directly with the text of Scripture, as over against Orthodox emphasis on reading the text within the context of Tradition (see Ch. 8) and together with all the faithful.

Orthodox and evangelicals alike would look to Christ, the living Word, as the source of Christian faith. Moving beyond such agreement to the means whereby the mind of Christ for his Church is discerned, and following the Reformers' insistence on 'Scripture alone', evangelicals hold the Bible as the final authority in all matters of faith and practice. The Orthodox likewise see Scripture as authoritative but also speak in terms of the authority of the Tradition[2] of the Church, of which Scripture is a part. Whereas evangelicals would insist that the individual conscience must be subject ultimately to Scripture, even when this results in conflict with churchly tradition, the Orthodox hold that Scripture can only be understood aright from within the framework of that tradition. Orthodoxy sets the apostolic witness within the framework of an unbroken stream of divine life flowing from God through Christ in the Spirit to the apostles and through the early Fathers into the Church's life throughout the centuries. There are important issues here, for the New Testament record itself both emerges from within the life or tradition of the early church and is itself the foremost evidence for that phenomenon. The interrelationship between Scripture and Tradition has been, and will continue to be, an important item in discussions.

The complexity of Evangelicalism is evident in the differing ways in which evangelicals relate to the Christian past. Many have espoused a 'remnant theology' (cf. 1 Kgs. 19:18; Mt. 24:12–13; Rom. 9:27–9, 11:5), in which God is seen as preserving a faithful minority in each generation of church history, often amid the wreckage and corruption of the visible church. Since the Pentecostal-charismatic sector, which has existed as a separate movement only in the twentieth century, is the fastest growing variety of evangelicalism (in the United Kingdom, it includes approximately two-thirds of the membership of the Evangelical Alliance), a greater part of Evangelicalism may be moving towards a mentality which seeks no validation beyond the New Testament. Most other strands of Evangelicalism recognize that they have received the faith only from the preceding millennia of church life, but no evangelical could readily subscribe to Orthodoxy's view of the history of the institutional church since the apostles as an unbroken continuum of divine life: indebtedness to the sixteenth-century Reformation makes most evangelicals more sharply aware of the fallibility and corruptibility of the Church.

Thinking of Tradition as the work of the Holy Spirit in human history is an Orthodox approach which has helped some evangelicals to see it more positively. A theology in which nothing happened between the closing of the canon and our own times is not defensible; one that shortens that period by restarting the story with the Reformers is hardly any better. For the Orthodox the Church is a continuity from apostolic times to the present without any new beginnings or new starts: it sees itself as the church which has never had (or needed) a Reformation, although renewal is recognized as a constant need.

The importance of Tradition for the Orthodox shows up in very practical ways. Take for example the offence given by an evangelical missionary addressing a group of Armenians and talking about how evangelical missionaries 'brought the gospel' to Armenia in the nineteenth century. Or consider how the Orthodox have spoken of the offensiveness that they find in Baptist notions of 'church planting' in Eastern Europe or Central Asia. In both cases it is as if, for all their history, they were perceived as pagan until evangelicals arrived on the scene. In such stances the Orthodox see the witness of the faithful in holding to the liturgy through years of trial and tribulation, along with the costly witness of their persecuted ancestors, counting for nothing. Careless talk is seen to de-church the faithful of past generations.

### iii) Evangelism and proselytism

The scale of such costly witness is critical to a sympathetic understanding of where Orthodox believers are coming from: their faith has a long history and due recognition of this is especially important. The Orthodox have struggled for existence alongside alien forces, whether militant Islam, Communism, or the materialism that has succeeded the downfall of Marxist ideology. The track record of the West in this story has not been good. Crusading soldiers in 1204 found the plunder of the riches of Byzantium a more attractive goal than the reconquest of lands under Muslim rule, and at various points Western missionaries, encountering the stubbornness of an Islamic mission field, have turned to the easier prospect of proselytizing faithful Orthodox.

Part of the story has also been the promotion of *uniatism* by the Catholic Church. From the twelfth century onwards the Vatican has allowed a number of communities in Eastern Europe to retain their own Eastern liturgical practices, canon law and the parochial ministry of married priests, on the one condition of accepting the primacy of the Pope. The Council of Ferrara/Florence (1438–45) insisted upon unity of faith while allowing the use of different liturgical rites. This policy has been seen by the Orthodox not as a form of ecumenical accommodation, but as a major way of proselytizing not just individuals but whole communities.

It is against this background that Protestant missionary endeavours have to be perceived. If Catholicism has exploited the vulnerability of Orthodoxy in the past, then Western Protestant missionaries are seen by many Orthodox as continuing in that tradition, with their unequal access to technological power and educational privilege and the lavish promises sometimes made to potential converts.[3]

Thus part of the problem of relationships has to do with conflicting histories. Within the Orthodox story, the very fact of *being* forms a significant part of witness, because *doing*, which (in the sense of evangelizing) evangelical missions have more readily identified as the essence of mission, has been so much circumscribed.

The story of Orthodox missions needs to be better known and understood by evangelicals, for it is ignorant to suggest that the Orthodox churches are lacking in a mission history of their own. Such ignorance has meant that in Alaska, for example, Protestant missionaries were unaware of the successful Orthodox mission there during the eighteenth and nineteenth centuries. It is unjust that Western mission agencies should stereotype Orthodoxy as 'anti-mission' and, worse than that, characterize all popular Orthodox practice as idolatrous, unbiblical, backward or lacking in spiritual depth.

On the other hand, evangelical groups in predominantly Orthodox countries point to state, and sometimes church, slander of their good name and even overt persecution. Well-documented incidents of evangelicals being threatened by mobs which have received encouragement from local Orthodox clerics, of evangelical churches and prayer houses being destroyed, and of evangelical groups being denied permission to register as legal entities,[4] led many Western evangelicals to take a sharply critical attitude towards Orthodoxy. This has a 'knock-on' effect upon relationships between evangelical missionaries and Orthodox communities in Eastern Europe. A number of factors impinge here. One is the Orthodox concept of canonical territories (traditionally, an Orthodox jurisdiction sees itself as *the* church in its geographical area) and the church's consequent difficulty in coming to terms with the religious pluralism so familiar in parts of the West, leading to the unchurching of other Christian groups. Another is that many evangelical groups resent the allegation that Evangelicalism is 'Western' or 'American'. Beyond this, the distinction between evangelicals and sectarians is not always made, leading to understandable evangelical hurt. Finally, an earlier history of persecution from state churches in Eastern Europe fuels continuing suspicion amongst evangelicals of any attempt to recreate the kind of church-state relationship which they believe would constitute a threat to their freedom of action.

When history is presented in this way, with stress laid on conflict and disagreement, there are very real difficulties in perceiving Tradition in church history as reflecting the work of the Holy Spirit. Whilst evangelical missionaries can never surrender to the Orthodox any idea of exclusive operation within given 'canonical' territories, they may be able to agree not to disturb the faith of the faithful who are regular in their attendance at the liturgy, and concentrate instead on unbelievers and those who have lapsed from regular participation in church life, as well as seeking to build up existing churches (see Ch. 11). This would require a significant shift in their evaluation of the spiritual status of both Orthodox and indigenous evangelical believers.

## iv) Worship and spirituality

Anyone who has experienced evangelical and Orthodox worship will be aware of considerable differences of practice (see Ch. 9). These include the contrast between the evangelical use of the vernacular and the deployment by some Orthodox jurisdictions of an ancient ecclesiastical language no longer in common use (in the light of the older Orthodox tradition of translating the Scriptures and the liturgy into local languages, this has been described as a 'blatant contradiction' by the Orthodox missiologist Ion Bria[5]). There is also the contrast between the flexible approach of many evangelicals to orders of service and the Orthodox insistence upon use of set forms. The evangelical pattern may seem very word-orientated, while the Orthodox, although deploying much Scriptural language, will focus more on symbol and action. Evangelical worship often climaxes in a verbal presentation of the gospel; Orthodox worship tends to lead into apprehension of mystery, heightened perhaps by the use of colour, chanting and incense. Ecclesiastical architecture provides further visible contrasts between the two worship styles (see Ch. 9).

In times of persecution Orthodoxy has found its strength, on the one hand, in the monastic tradition with its ministry of prayer and compassionate service; and, on the other, in the home – thus, the importance of the witness of the grandmothers who maintained the faith and its traditions in many Russian families during the long period of Soviet oppression. For its part, Evangelicalism has close connections historically with Pietism, which stressed cultivation of personal piety and service by all Christians. It too has cultivated the religion of the family.

## v) Conversion, salvation and deification

The language used and the stresses made when talking about salvation are evidence of the very different theological cultures of Evangelicalism and Orthodoxy. The same terms may be used with very different meanings, while the same meaning may be expressed by a different set of terms. Great caution is therefore needed.

Nevertheless, this is an arena where further conversation could bring greater consensus. Areas of difference may be expressed in a series of questions:

- Is Christianity more a matter of individual decision or of community-based faith expression?
- What is the relation between birth and second birth?
- Is conversion to be seen as a single event or a continuing process?
- Is spirituality a matter of inner religious experience or a more holistic change of lifestyle?
- Theologically, is it right to speak in terms of atonement and justification, or of deification★ (*theosis*★)?
- How does justification relate to sanctification – and how can both be related to Orthodox language of deification?
- What does it mean to speak of salvation as being received in and through the Church?
- In all these, what is the relationship between the divine initiative and human response, between grace, faith and works (and how are those terms understood)?

Does Charles Wesley's plea in one of his hymns, 'Change my nature into thine',[6] suggest that there could be convergence of understanding? Reflection on 2 Peter 1:4 would seem to lead in a similar direction, for the apostle writes, '[Christ] has given us his very great and precious promises, so that through them you may participate in the divine nature.' The language of deification was used by Reformers such as Luther and Calvin, although it is not as prominent in their thinking as it is in Orthodox theology. Perhaps consensus could be achieved here similar to that which already exists in agreeing on the need for the blood of Christ to be shed in atonement for sin and in affirming that the supreme sacrifice of the incarnate Christ represents the only way to salvation.

The debate about the nature of salvation will also have implications for debate about the nature of the Church. The Orthodox work with an inclusive model, based on all those baptized (often in infancy, and with little evidence of continuing commitment) being regarded as church members.[7] While some evangelicals would share this approach, many work on a more exclusive model, in which church membership is defined by a deliberate commitment by the individual to be Christ's disciple, which entails commitment to one's fellow Christians in the corporate life of the local church.[8] In practice, many Orthodox in the East shared this approach to a certain extent, since only the committed would be prepared to make the sacrifices called for by public religious profession under an anti-religious government.

## vi) Sacramental theology

Since the eighteenth century, many evangelicals have seen ecclesiology as a secondary issue, and there has often been a corresponding lack of emphasis on the sacraments. By contrast, the Orthodox see the sacraments as an essential nourishing of the believer with the grace needed to tread the way of salvation, although there have not been lacking those such as St Symeon the New Theologian (949–1022) who stressed the fundamental importance of inward transformation, without which no sacrament could convey any spiritual benefit.

### a) Baptism and discipleship

When an Orthodox priest declares a newly baptized baby to be a Christian, he is really saying that the child has begun to become a Christian. Salvation is conceived of as a process, though a process initially dependent upon the work of Christ. The process begins at baptism and is continued through faith, repentance and all the disciplines of the Christian life. Orthodox thought tends to treat all these as a package, and so does not make the clear distinctions made by evangelicals between justification, sanctification and glorification.

Baptism for the Orthodox is the sacrament of initiation into the kingdom of God and the life of the Church. Sometimes that has been compromised by baptism being seen as also constituting initiation into the life of the community, so that questions of ethnicity have been confused with questions of church identity. In the West, too, this aspect of medieval thinking was carried over by Reformers such as Ulrich Zwingli (1484–1531) and Luther. Clearly, evangelical missions find a difficulty with this view of baptism, if it is seen to constrain evangelical endeavour amongst the nominal or lapsed members in Orthodox canonical territories, for it then becomes a firm instruction to 'keep off the grass', forbidding evangelical missionaries to enter a given geographical area. More positively, baptism may be seen by the Orthodox as well as evangelicals as a commissioning for service in mission in allegiance to the risen Christ. Also, a need for more effective post-baptismal instruction (*catechesis*) is widely recognized by the Orthodox.

Historically, evangelicals have adopted a broad range of views about baptism. Many have embraced paedobaptism (the baptism of infants). Among these, Lutherans accept infant baptismal regeneration. Some Calvinists have accepted that God may choose to regenerate elect infants in baptism; most would see baptism as incorporating the baptized person (infant or adult) into the visible church, and would justify this view by analogy with the role played by circumcision in the Old Covenant. On the other hand, Baptist evangelicals have been marked out by their insistence that baptism should be given only on profession of faith. This view is often misunderstood (even by many Baptists) as 'adult baptism'. However, other Baptists have accepted that no strict age limit can be imposed; a young child who makes a credible profession of faith could be baptized. Thus in some Baptist churches in America, quite young children are baptized on confession of their faith. Baptists have also tended to treat baptism as embodying primarily the human response to God's grace, whereas evangelical paedobaptists see it as expressing primarily the divine initiative of grace (which is one factor that makes it appropriate to baptize an infant). The mode of baptism varies among evangelicals from immersion (the usual Baptist practice) to affusion or sprinkling (more common among paedobaptists).

Fresh ecumenical reflection on baptism, especially in the light of a growing recognition that baptism following confession of faith should be regarded as the normative pattern, has been taking place in most major Christian traditions. The Orthodox and evangelicals would profit from sharing more fully in this process, and from considering together the place which they believe baptism holds in Christian initiation.

## b) The Liturgy

Nowadays, a substantial proportion of evangelical Eucharistic theology tends to be memorialist, a dramatic re-presentation in symbolic action of the death and resurrection of Jesus. Certainly that which is signified is always seen as more important than the sign that recalls it. By contrast, the Orthodox believe the actual body and blood of Christ to be present in the consecrated bread and wine. Clearly, that this should be so, is a mystery: Orthodoxy has generally resisted any attempt to define how it happens. But mystery is what the Liturgy is all about: seeing the present moment in time and all human experience in relation to the larger dimension of eternity and its realities. For the Orthodox, it is an opportunity for a re-presentation of the once-for-all incarnation, crucifixion and resurrection of Jesus, just as the Passover meal enabled Jews to recapitulate the event when the angel of God passed over the specially identified homes of the faithful. In celebrating the Eucharist, the Orthodox believe that the Church is most truly itself, in communion with all the faithful of every age, and in communion through the Holy Spirit with the Father and the Son.

Whilst to many evangelicals the form of the Liturgy may seem very strange, many of the emphases of the service are Trinitarian, Christocentric and biblical (see Ch. 9). For the average evangelical the sermon is a major focus within worship, which has often been heavily cerebral in its form; although the sermon is also important to some Orthodox, it is the action of the Eucharist which forms the climax of the Liturgy.

The action of the Liturgy may seem remote from everyday life, but relating its content and action to daily life is an important imperative. In this respect the concept of 'The liturgy after the Liturgy' has proved to be a fruitful way of describing mission obligations in terms which make a natural appeal to Orthodox believers (see Ch. 11). This phrase, which draws on the thought of St John Chrysostom (c. 349–407), refers to the inter-relationship between the gathering of God's people at the Eucharist to offer praise and receive his grace, and their scattering throughout the world, renewed by participation in the Liturgy, to glorify God in all aspects of human life and thus serve as agents of the divine purpose of liberation which is manifested in the Liturgy proper.[9]

## vii) Theological method

Underlying many of the differences between evangelicals and the Orthodox is the fact that they have radically different approaches to doing theology. Thus dialogue must not be allowed to degenerate into an exchange of Bible texts because they may, in the different theological and philosophical frameworks of Evangelicalism and Orthodoxy, be taken to mean quite different things. A full explanation of the differences between these frameworks would entail providing an account of the development of the whole Western theological tradition during the medieval period, and in particular an evaluation of the significance of Augustine of Hippo (354–430) for the development of Western theology, well beyond the scope of the present exercise. It would also entail an account of the way in which the Eastern theological tradition was shaped by its encounter with different phases of Platonic philosophy, especially Neoplatonism. Suffice it here to sketch out the different approaches adopted by evangelicals and the Orthodox today.

Evangelicals have always stressed the importance of God's

revelation as propositional in nature. Consequently their message emphasizes what can be known about God. Although they acknowledge the impossibility of knowing everything about God, they would nevertheless affirm that because he has revealed himself to humankind in the events of salvation history (most notably by becoming man in the incarnation) and in Scripture as the God-breathed (divinely inspired) and trustworthy witness to his saving acts, men and women can have a knowledge of God which, though partial, is still true. Such knowledge cannot be absorbed by human intelligence unaided: 'to read, mark, learn and inwardly digest' such a revelation requires the aid of the illuminating Spirit to dispel human ignorance.

The Orthodox speak of two ways of doing theology, *kataphatic* and *apophatic*. The first emphasizes what can be known; the second what cannot be known. We must declare what we know of God, but in the end we must balance this with the recognition that God is so far beyond human comprehension that it is easier to say what (or who) God is not than to say what (or who) God is. The experience of God is one which passes understanding; ultimately, knowing God is not a matter of intellectual comprehension, but of experiential union through prayer and contemplation. This may explain why Orthodoxy has perhaps been more successful than modern Evangelicalism in maintaining a strong link between theology and spiritual experience, between the propositional and the personal aspects of Christianity. It is not that evangelicals would deny the importance of such a link, but that contemporary evangelical practice (unlike that of many in earlier generations) has often fallen somewhat short of the ideal.

## viii) Conclusion

Clearly these are weighty matters, and discussion will require both a willingness to speak honestly and a readiness to listen humbly to the views of others. Careful interpretation is also needed, in view of the different theological languages which we speak. Dialogue which papers over the cracks is limited in what it can achieve; it is better to seek to learn from one another, repentant for past misunderstanding and committed to obeying the Spirit of Truth who will lead us into all truth (Jn. 16:13).

## Notes

1 For a report of this meet, see Huibert van Beek and Georges Lemopoulos (eds.), *Proclaiming Christ Today: Orthodox – Evangelical Consultation, Alexandria, 10–15 July 1995* (Geneva/Białystok: World Council of Churches/ Syndesmos, 1995).

2 Tradition is here spelt with a capital T to distinguish it from many less essential traditions within Orthodox thought and practice; for more detail concerning this distinction, see Ch. 8.

3 In fairness, this negative assessment needs to be balanced by recogntion of the sacrificial work of many missionaries, notably those who are themselves from Eastern Europe. For a careful assessment of the mistakes made by Western missionaries in post-Communist Russia, along with some suggestions for good practice, see Lawrence A. Uzzell, 'Guidelines for American Missionaries in Russia', in John Witte, Jr and Michael Bourdeaux (eds), *Proselytism and Orthodoxy in Russia* (Maryknoll, NY: Orbis, 1999), pp. 323–30.

4 The Keston Institute (4 Park Town, Oxford, OX2 6SH; e-mail: keston.institute@keston.org) provides a regular digest of news concerning issues related to religious freedom; see their monthly publication *Keston News Service* and their magazine *Frontier*, as well as their academic journal *Religion, State and Society* (formerly *Religion in Communist Lands*).

5 Ion Bria, *The Liturgy after the Liturgy* (Geneva: World Council of Churches, 1996), p. 23.

6 From his hymn 'Since the Son hath made me free', *Methodist Hymn Book* (London: Methodist Conference Office, 1933), no. 568.

7 Many Orthodox also adopt an inclusive approach in considering the status of non-Orthodox Christians; a minority go further, applying this approach in their consideration of adherents of other faiths. See Ch. 7 for further consideration of the inclusive nature of Orthodox ecclesiology.

8 However, Evangelicalism does not insist that the salvation requires membership of a particular denomination tradition.

9 For fuller exposition see Ion Bria, 'The Liturgy after the Liturgy', in Gennadios Limouris (ed.), *Orthodox Visions of Ecumenism: Statements, Messages and Reports on the Ecumenical Movement 1902–1992* (Geneva: World Council of Churches, 1994), pp. 216–20, as well as the same author's book *The Liturgy after the Liturgy*, referred to earlier.

# 5

# The Person and Work of Christ

The Person of Christ is a mystery. This is the first and most important point to emphasize when speaking of Christ and salvation. On this Orthodox and evangelicals would agree, although the latter may not be used to expressing it in those terms. Indeed the meaning of *any* person's being is knowable only in glimpses (cf. Ps. 139:1–16). How much more a mystery, therefore, is the Person of Jesus Christ, the incarnate Son of God.

Yet the Person of Christ is also a *revealed* mystery. The New Testament use of *mysterion* concerns precisely a mystery that has been revealed with the incarnation of the Son of God (cf. Rom 16:25; Col. 1:26–27; 1 Tim. 3:16). Thus, while retaining a powerful sense of the ultimate unknowability of Christ, the Orthodox have an equally powerful sense that all creation has been affected by the incarnation and therefore that everything material now carries with it the potential to be restored to perfection, as it was when God created it. Salvation is 'essentially . . . the restoration of man and the world to their original state'.[1] Evangelicals would not disagree with this, although traditionally they have laid more stress on certainty than upon mystery. This is one reason why they have constantly tried to frame their understanding of their faith in confessions which are often much more detailed than the early creeds. A key to understanding Evangelicalism is to understand its emphasis on the centrality of Christ, particularly with regard to his work on the cross. Of course, an Orthodox would have no problems affirming the saving significance of the cross or an evangelical the importance of the incarnation; indeed, evangelicals have been rediscovering the vitality that a strong belief in the incarnation brings to Christian faith.

There are several ways in which the subject of the Person and work of Christ in Orthodoxy and Evangelicalism might be tackled. We might look at the scriptural texts given particular emphasis during the festivals of the church year, although this could exclude non-liturgical evangelicals. Or we might look at the Christological statements made by the early councils and accepted as authoritative. The Nicene Creed is proclaimed at every Orthodox baptism and Eucharist (and at other services too) and many Orthodox include it as part of their daily prayers. It is recited at Anglican Communion services too, and together with the Apostles' Creed has prominence in Anglican and Methodist worship, and some place in Presbyterian worship also. Again, such a focus would probably exclude those evangelicals from 'independent' traditions, such as Baptists and Pentecostals. Most evangelicals within these traditions would be unfamiliar with the early creeds, although they would readily recognize much if not all of their teaching as Scriptural.[2] Alternatively, it would be possible to look at what the authoritative teachers of the Church ('the Fathers') have to say about the Person of Christ and salvation. However, many Orthodox, as well as the majority of evangelicals, would be unfamiliar with teachers such as St Athanasius or St Basil. We shall therefore approach the subject by looking at the worship life of the Orthodox Church. Faithful Orthodox will have been nurtured by what they have heard in church, even though they may also be familiar with the Fathers or the teaching of Scripture; similarly, evangelicals will have had their theology shaped by what they sing, singing being arguably the most significant 'liturgical' activity for many strands of Evangelicalism. While this approach will not produce a systematic theology, it may be most appropriate for a mystery caught in glimpses.

## i) The Person and Work of Christ in Orthodoxy

Every service in an Orthodox church reflects its Christology and soteriology. We shall examine the central prayer of the baptismal rite as an example of an Orthodox approach to these themes. The same prayer is adapted for use at the 'Great Blessing of Waters', on the feast of Theophany, which in the Christian East from ancient times was the feast of the incarnation.

Whether the person is an adult or a child, the baptismal rite is the same. For the Orthodox, full inclusion of children (and mentally handicapped) in the life in Christ reflects a view of communion with God that goes beyond rational acceptance of confessions of faith and reflects as well a deep sense that Christian life is fundamentally communal. It is also significant that the rite itself is couched in terms which envisage an adult as the baptismal candidate, and it preserves a confession of faith that presupposes the candidate's decision to accept Christ and join the Church. This reflects the origins of the rite at a time (the fourth century) when most people being baptized were adults; now, most Orthodox baptisms are of infants. Without going into the details, it is instructive to see what confession of faith is expected.

*The sponsors with the child (or adult) . . . stand facing the priest. The priest asks them three times:*
Do you unite yourself to Christ? *I do unite myself to Christ.*
Have you united yourself to Christ? *I have united myself to Christ.*
Do you believe in him? *I believe in Him as King and God.* (This is followed by confession of the Nicene Creed.)
*After the Creed, the priest makes the following inquiry three times:*
Have you united yourself to Christ?
*The candidate or sponsor responds each time:* I have united myself to Christ.
**Priest:** Bow down before him.
**Candidate or sponsor (bowing):** I bow down before the Father, and the Son, and the Holy Spirit, the Trinity, one in essence and undivided.
**Priest:** Blessed is God who desires that all people be saved and come to the knowledge of the truth, now and ever and unto ages of ages!
**People:** Amen.

**Priest:** Let us pray to the Lord.

**People:** Lord have mercy.

**Priest:** O Master, Lord our God, call thy servant (name) to thy holy Illumination and grant him (her) that great grace of thy holy Baptism. Put off from him (her) the old man, and renew him (her) unto life everlasting; and fill him (her) with the power of thy Holy Spirit, in the unity of thy Christ: that he (she) may be no more a child of the body, but a child of thy Kingdom. Through the good will and grace of thine Only-begotten Son, with whom thou art blessed, together with thy most holy, and good and life-creating Spirit, now and ever and unto ages of ages.

**People:** Amen. . . .

*The priest then blesses the water by dipping the fingers of his right hand into it and tracing the Sign of the Cross three times. He breathes on the water and says:*

Let all adverse powers be crushed beneath the sign of the image of thy Cross. (repeated three times). We pray thee, O God, that every aerial and obscure phantom may withdraw itself from us; and that no demon of darkness may conceal himself in this water; and that no evil spirit which instills darkening of intentions and rebelliousness of thought may descend into it with him (her) who is about to be baptised.

But do thou, O Master of all, show this water to be the water of redemption, the water of sanctification, the purification of flesh and spirit, the loosing of bonds, the remission of sins, the illumination of the soul, the bath of regeneration, the renewal of the Spirit, the gift of adoption to sonship, the garment of incorruption, the fountain of life. For thou, O Lord, hast said: Wash and be clean; put away evil things from your souls. Thou hast bestowed upon us from on high a new birth through water and the Spirit. Wherefore, O Lord, manifest thyself in this water, and grant that he (she) who is baptised therein may be transformed; that he (she) may put away from him (her) the old man which is corrupt through the lusts of the flesh, and that he (she) may be clothed with the new man, and renewed after the image of him who created him (her): that being buried, after the pattern of thy death, in baptism, he (she) may, in like manner, be a partaker of thy resurrection; and having preserved the gift of the Holy Spirit, and increased the measure of grace committed unto him (her) he (she) may receive the prize of his (her) high calling, and be numbered with the first-born whose names are written in heaven, in thee, our God and Lord, Jesus Christ.

For unto thee are due glory, dominion, honour and worship, together with thy Father, who is from everlasting, and thine all-holy, and good and life-giving Spirit, now and ever and unto ages of ages.

**People:** Amen.

Even from this cursory glance at Orthodox worship, the Christological and soteriological dimensions are clear, and an evangelical will also recognize the tightly packed Pauline and Johannine imagery in this service:

- Christ is confessed as God, as the only-begotten Son of God, as the second Person of the Trinity. In the Nicene Creed his true humanity is also affirmed.

- Baptism is seen as the beginning of the process of inner transformation, not because it possesses magical efficacy but because in it the Holy Spirit is active. This beginning is also described as 'new birth' and as burial and resurrection. The process of transformation involves freedom from spiritual slavery, forgiveness of sins, illumination of the soul, spiritual regeneration, renewal in the image of God and adoption as a child of God. The goal is to become a 'child of the kingdom', to be numbered with those whose names are written in heaven. To that end, the individual is responsible to put off the old man and put on the new, and to preserve the gift of the Spirit committed to him/her. A balance is thus maintained between divine agency and human responsibility.

- A constantly recurring motif is that of *life*; Orthodox teaching concerning sin stresses not only that it represents breaking a divine command, but also that it brings in its wake alienation from God and death, physical and spiritual. It is a disease which, if left untreated, will result in death. Adam's sin brought

death into the world, and death is what causes us to sin. What
we have inherited is not sinfulness but mortality. It is thus
death, even more than sin, which Christ came to defeat.[3] In
this light, it will readily be understood why the Orthodox
place so much stress on Christ's resurrection, which they see as
guaranteeing the resurrection of believers at his Second
Coming but also as conferring resurrection life upon them
here and now. Easter (or *Pascha*) is the major festival in the
Orthodox year, and the occasion for vivid re-presentation of
the resurrection of Christ. Christ is the one who 'trampled
down death by death' and brought 'light to those in the
tombs'.

● Christ's death on the cross is seen as having defeated the evil
powers, but little else is said about it here; the Creed merely
states that he was crucified 'for us'. Orthodox thought is often
content to affirm that Christ's death was both a sacrifice and a
victory, without inquiring too deeply into how it is that we
benefit thereby. Underlying patristic thinking concerning the
work of Christ is the belief that 'what is not assumed is not
healed', that Christ had to take our human nature in order that
he might redeem it and that we might share in his divine
nature. The death of Christ is confessed in a liturgical setting
rather than analyzed in the face of challenges to Orthodox
belief. It is the resurrection which tends to receive greater
emphasis.

## ii) The Person and Work of Christ in Evangelicalism

By contrast with Orthodoxy, it is symptomatic of the breadth of
Evangelicalism that no one service could be offered to demonstrate
its understanding of Christ and salvation. Rather, we may look at
evangelical hymnody as a means of grasping its theology, since this
has a similar formative role. Consider, for example, the following
hymns:

**Let earth and heaven combine,**
angels and men agree
to praise in songs divine
th'incarnate Deity,
our God contracted to a span,
incomprehensibly made man.

He laid his glory by,
he wrapped him in our clay,
unmarked by human eye
the latent Godhead lay:
infant of days he here became,
and bore the loved Immanuel's name. . . .

He deigns in flesh to appear,
widest extremes to join,
to bring our vileness near,
and make us all-divine;
and we the life of God shall know,
for God is manifest below.

Made perfect first in love,
and sanctified by grace,
we shall from earth remove
and see his glorious face;
his love shall then be fully showed,
and man shall then be lost in God.[4]

**Here is love, vast as the ocean,**
Lovingkindness as the flood,
When the Prince of life, our ransom,
Shed for us his precious blood.
Who his love will not remember?
Who can cease to sing his praise?
He can never be forgotten
Throughout heaven's eternal days.

On the mount of crucifixion
Fountains opened deep and wide;
Through the floodgates of God's mercy
Flowed a vast and gracious tide.
Grace and love, like mighty rivers,
Poured incessant from above,
And heaven's peace and perfect justice
Kissed a guilty world in love.[5]

Many more such items, old and new, could be quoted as expressing the core Christological and soteriological beliefs outlined in Chapter One. What they show us is a robust classical Christology (especially evident in the older hymns) which strikes the familiar notes of Christ's true deity and humanity.

The *Person* of Christ, then, does not represent a divisive issue between Orthodoxy and Evangelicalism. However, the *work* of Christ, and the way in which his Person and his work are related, are altogether trickier subjects. Both traditions would accept the classical affirmations concerning Christ's two natures (human and divine), his virgin birth, perfect holiness, atoning death, resurrection, ascension and his coming again in glory. In the evangelical hymns quoted above, we find a soteriology which is rather richer than might be expected. Soteriological parallels between the two traditions also appear: in terms of how Christ's saving work benefits us, there are clear affirmations not only of forgiveness of sins and removal of guilt, but also of the goal of salvation as being human perfection and participation in the life of God. Contrary to a common misperception of evangelical belief, the whole work of salvation is rooted in and expressive of the *love* of God (cf. Evangelicalism's love of Jn. 3:16).

It is true that certain aspects of soteriology are rather more extensively developed in Evangelicalism than in Orthodoxy: evangelical hymnody as a whole displays a definite preference for the substitutionary model of the atonement. However, other models are also used (the 'Christus Victor' model, which interprets the death and resurrection of Christ as conquering the powers of evil, has been particularly popular in modern charismatic songs), and such items as those above also assign saving significance to the incarnation. Indeed, it could even be said that popular Evangelicalism has been shaped in part by patristic thought, through the medium of Charles Wesley's hymns. The Wesleys were significantly influenced by the theology of the Fathers, to which they would have been introduced by the writings of seventeenth-century Anglican thinkers such as Lancelot Andrewes (1555–1626) and Thomas Ken (1637–1710). Thus there is a patristic strain of Christological and soteriological thought at the heart of evangelical worship.

However, the atoning death of Christ as a substitute for sinners is pivotal to the evangelical view of salvation in a way that it is not for Orthodox (though it is present in patristic thought). Evangelicals, particularly in the English-speaking world, place a far greater emphasis on the cross than on the incarnation. In terms of the application of the work of Christ to the individual, evangelicals affirm the doctrine of justification by faith as fundamental to their understanding of what it means to become a Christian. If the Orthodox want to understand Evangelicalism as a movement, this doctrine is the place to start.

The doctrine of justification by grace alone through faith alone can rightly be considered primary among evangelical beliefs. Rooted in scriptural passages such as Ephesians 2:8–9 and Romans 3 – 8, it is a belief which can be traced within all strands of Evangelicalism. It was the battle cry of Protestant Reformers such as Luther (whose followers described it as 'the article by which a church stands or falls'), Melanchthon, Calvin (who called it 'the main hinge on which religion turns'), Cranmer and Knox. The soteriological heart of the Reformation lay in the careful distinction the Reformers made between justification (God's declaration that the believer is accepted as righteous for Christ's sake) and sanctification (the Holy Spirit's work of renewal within the believer). Note, however, that this was a distinction, and not a separation: Calvin in particular was careful to safeguard this by his doctrine of the union of the believer with Christ by the Spirit, justification and sanctification (which he termed 'regeneration') being seen as consequences of this,[6] while John Wesley stressed the need for faith to be active through love (Gal. 5:6). The belief that salvation is solely by grace and not by works was also central to the theology of movements such as the Baptists, and it is one of the most prominent doctrines found in traditional evangelical hymns. In short then, the doctrine is fundamental to evangelical identity: an individual can come into relationship with God without having to perform any act or work as a precondition. For evangelicals, salvation is by means of grace alone. Orthodox would say this too, but as well as combining this with a clear statement of human freedom to respond to God's grace they would stress the use of the sacraments as channels of grace, whereas many non-Lutheran and non-Anglican evangelicals today regard grace as operating apart from sacraments.

This emphasis on the freeness of grace has sometimes led to evangelicals appearing to be careless about good works; more fundamentally for relationships and discussions with Orthodox Christians, it means that the Orthodox emphasis on human endeavour can seem like 'righteousness by good works' to evangelicals. This suspicion is due in part to misunderstanding, but some Orthodox theology does provide evidence for such an interpretation. Perhaps we may summarize the differences in approach by saying that evangelical teaching urges us to engage in good works *because* we have been accepted by God (justified), while Orthodox teaching tends to speak of doing good works *in order that* we may be accepted on the last day. Recent debate concerning Paul's understanding of such concepts as justification, law and works, and the nature of the relationship between them in first-century Jewish thinking, may have thrown up some potentially fruitful lines of inquiry for further dialogue to pursue.[7]

### iii) Comparison and contrast

For both evangelicals and Orthodox, salvation is ultimately about union with Christ, and through him with the Father and the Holy Spirit. However, in the Orthodox liturgical excerpt above, beliefs are expressed with which many evangelicals would be uncomfortable, notably concerning the regenerative efficacy of baptism. There are also aspects of evangelical theology, especially at the popular level, which the Orthodox would regard as aberrant. Some significant areas of disagreement are noted below:

1. Evangelicalism is certainly Trinitarian, but it is worth making the point that there are times when evangelicals centre on Christ at the expense of the first and third Persons of the Trinity; this has drawn criticism from Orthodox writers. Charismatics likewise are on occasion guilty of focusing on the Spirit at the expense of the

he Son. Both find it hard to absorb the threeness of the
their thinking.

2. What would shake an evangelical is the apparent absence of a
stress on the cross in this excerpt from the baptismal service. In fact,
the Orthodox are more likely to speak of cross and resurrection in
the same breath. For them baptism is the act of a person's death and
resurrection in and with Jesus. Christian baptism is our participation
in the event of Easter. It is a new birth by water and the Holy Spirit
into the Kingdom of God (cf. Jn. 3:5). For the evangelical, reference
would of necessity be made to St Paul's observation that in baptism
the candidate dies, is buried and is raised to new life; in that
connection it is noteworthy that the epistle read at Orthodox
baptisms is Romans 6:3–11, a favourite passage for preachers at
evangelical baptismal services.

The Orthodox sometimes criticize evangelical theology because
it appears to assign no significant purpose to the resurrection apart
from saying that Christ rose from the dead to prove the truth of his
claims to divinity, or that his resurrection represented a victory over
the powers of evil. The Orthodox would agree with these, but also
stress that Christ rose from the dead so that we, being united with
him, might share in his risen life. Evangelicals, on the other hand,
might feel that Orthodoxy undervalues the considerable amount of
biblical material underlying the substitutionary model of the
atonement (e.g. Lev. 16; Is. 53:4–12; Gal. 3:13; 1 Pet. 2:24, 3:18), and
that it is too quick to write this model off as 'legalistic' without
recognizing, firstly, that it is clearly present in Scripture and,
secondly, that evangelical preachers (and classic evangelical hymns
and liturgies) delight to set it in the context of the love of a God
who purposes to enter into a personal relationship with sinners (cf.
Jn. 3.16; Rom. 5:8). Related to this is a difference of emphasis
concerning the nature of human alienation from God: evangelicals
tend to give a much more prominent place to sin as the
fundamental cause of this alienation, regarding death as a
consequence of sin (cf. Rom. 5:12-19 as traditionally understood in
the West), whereas the Orthodox often put things the other way

round. Moreover, evangelicals would often take a more radical view of the devastating effects of sin on the human make-up: many would say that it has vitiated every part of human nature.

3. Soteriology and Christology are related differently in the two traditions. The Protestant Reformers affirmed Chalcedonian Christology, with its emphasis on the two natures of Christ as truly God and truly man, since this was essential if he was to act as mediator. In the eleventh century, Anselm of Canterbury produced a classic Western statement of this in his *Cur Deus Homo* (*Why God became Man*). The Reformers' focus was very much on what Christ came to *do*, and this has been understood primarily in terms of his dealing with sin through his obedience as the last Adam, culminating in his substitutionary death. The incarnation was thus necessary if the Son of God was to live and die in the place of sinful human beings.

In the Eastern tradition, the picture is somewhat different, prominence being given to what Christ came to *be*. Indeed, it is often said that the incarnation would still be necessary even if man had never fallen into sin. Thus the Orthodox today are much more likely than evangelicals to assign primary saving significance to the incarnation. For them, Christ reconciled God and man chiefly by becoming man; by incorporation into Christ, therefore, there is opened up to believers the prospect of union with God or *theosis*.

Each tradition could study the way in which soteriology and Christology are related by the other. In particular, evangelicals could consider what the incarnation implies about the nature of salvation and of God's relationship with his creation, while the Orthodox could reflect on what the cross says about the nature of God, and of our alienation from God.

4. Evangelicals believe that salvation is received by means of grace in a personal relationship with Christ through faith. Therefore many would struggle with the Orthodox veneration of icons or relics, and the idea that baptism effects regeneration. Many Orthodox will want to ask evangelicals how they can flourish as Christians without recourse to such elements as icons and relics: material elements

which, as a result of the sanctification of matter through the incarnation, are able to mediate a sense of the divine (though the extent to which the Orthodox use these does vary). The evangelical answer that Christians have this immediacy from their relationship with God in Christ through the Spirit would bewilder an Orthodox.

5. Many evangelicals would also raise their eyebrows at the Orthodox conception of *theosis*.[8] This is perhaps because they misunderstand what an Orthodox means by it. For the Orthodox it draws on Paul's teaching about sanctification and being 'in Christ', of being 'filled to the measure of all the fulness of God' (Eph. 3:19). They emphasize that full sharing of God's life is the ultimate aim of salvation (see Ch. 10). As one of the prayers following communion says, 'Grant that we may more perfectly partake of Thee in the never-ending day of Thy Kingdom.' It could be said that *theosis* is about the Christian's calling to become a child of the kingdom. In fact, it is arguable that in its broadest sense, the evangelical understanding of salvation has significant similarities to the Orthodox concept of *theosis* as ontological transformation (i.e. a transformation of the human nature of believers), since it asserts that God's purpose is to restore his image in us which was defaced by the Fall, transforming us into the likeness of Christ and enabling us to share in his immortality. Both traditions would agree, then, that the gospel is about God's provision of life for believing sinners.

6. Finally, evangelicals would not normally put as great an emphasis on the act of joining the Church as part of the process by which we are saved (see Ch. 7). This does not mean that membership of a local fellowship is not regarded as essential to Christian discipleship by most evangelicals – indeed it is – but somehow in their thinking this stands outside the salvation process. In theory, evangelicals would not want to separate Christ from the Church – but in practice many do. Much of this stems from the evangelical emphasis on the individual's relationship with God (see Ch. 10). By contrast, the Orthodox tend to understand salvation in a way which places greater weight on its corporate aspect. We might characterize the

two positions by saying that whereas Evangelicalism approaches the Church through Christ, Orthodoxy approaches Christ in the Church.

There are deeply held suspicions on both sides over each other's understanding of how we obtain salvation. Nevertheless, our understandings of Christ and of the nature of salvation (what he has saved us from and to) coalesce to a considerable degree. This should provide grounds for hope in evangelical-Orthodox conversations.


## Notes

1 S. Agourides, 'Salvation according to the Orthodox Tradition', *Ecumenical Review* 21 (1969), p. 192.

2 Some would have hesitations over expressions such as 'one baptism for the remission of sins' (because they would reject baptismal regeneration) or over calling the Church 'catholic' (which they would interpret as 'Roman').

3 See the clear exposition by Gerald Bray in J. I. Packer (ed.), *Here we Stand* (London: Hodder & Stoughton, 1986), pp. 104–6.

4 By Charles Wesley (1707–88).

5 William Rees (1802–83), translated from Welsh by William Edwards (1848–1929).

6 Recent Finnish Luther scholarship has sought to demonstrate that Luther also had a developed understanding of a real union of the believer with Christ; see Carl E. Braaten and Robert W. Jenson (eds), *Union with Christ: The New Finnish Interpretation of Luther* (Grand Rapids, MI/ Cambridge: Eerdmans, 1998). A major impetus towards this has been dialogue between Lutherans and Orthodox in Finland and elsewhere. Whether the attempt has been successful is debated.

7 For an accessible presentation of the issues, see Tom Wright, *What Saint Paul Really Said* (Oxford: Lion, 1997).

8 For a thorough examination of this crucial concept as developed by the Romanian Orthodox theologian Dumitriu Staniloae, see Emil Bartos, *Deification in Eastern Orthodox Theology* (Carlisle: Paternoster, 1999). Bartos is a Romanian Baptist.

# 6

# The Holy Spirit

The subject of the Holy Spirit in Evangelicalism and Orthodoxy has enormous potential both for renewal and division. Yet arguably evangelicals and Orthodox have much to contribute to each other.

## i) The Holy Spirit in the New Testament

In formulating their understanding of the Person and work of the Holy Spirit, evangelicals usually start with the New Testament, which is full of the stories of the Spirit and the early Christian missions, promised in the Gospels, recorded in Acts and expounded in the writings of St Paul. The Orthodox do this too but like their mentor, St Basil of Caesarea, they would want to insist that particular attention be paid to the activity of the Spirit in the incarnate Christ. He overshadows Mary, the maiden of Israel, enabling her to become nothing less than the *theotokos* – the bearer of the God–Man Jesus (Lk. 1:35). He drives the Lord Jesus into the desert to fast and wrestle with the Devil's temptations (Mk. 1:12). The God who affirms the Lord Jesus as his Son at the waters of baptism also anoints him with the Spirit (Mt. 3:16; Jn. 1:32). The Son of God become Son of Man does many mighty deeds in the power of the Spirit. St Paul tells us that this same Spirit raised Jesus from the dead (Rom. 8:11). In all his dealings in the life and death of Jesus the Spirit remains hidden from view: the evangelical J. I.

Packer even speaks of the Spirit's floodlight ministry, focusing on Christ.[1]

The Spirit is not, unlike the Lord Jesus, directly called *theos* ('God') anywhere in the New Testament (though he is identified with God in Acts 5:4, and elsewhere called *kyrios*, 'Lord'); but he clearly seems to belong in the closest possible relationship to God the Father and Jesus the Son of God. Not only is this evident in the baptismal narratives, but it is from the lips of Jesus Himself (Mt. 28:19) that the apostles are told to make disciples of the nations by baptizing them in the name of the Father and the Son and the Holy Spirit.

## ii) The Holy Spirit in early thought

Probably the best way to approach Orthodox thought on the Holy Spirit is through outlining the teaching of the Fathers. Indeed, the Orthodox have argued that the Ecumenical Councils, in which certain Fathers played prominent roles, can themselves be viewed as charismatic in nature; it was of the Council of Jerusalem, often quoted by the Orthodox as the precedent for such gatherings, that the apostles could say, 'It seemed good to the Holy Spirit and to us' (Acts 15:28).

Battles with error led to the need for these councils to engage in ever more precise definition. The historical evidence suggests that the early church took well over three hundred years to come to a mature understanding of the Spirit as expressed in the Nicene Creed, mainly because theologians were too caught up in Christological controversies to pay close attention to the third member of the Trinity. In recognizing the threat of ideas which subordinated the Spirit to the Son and the Father, St Irenaeus had emphasized that the Son and the Spirit are inherent in the very life of the Father; the Council of Nicea, however, had made no reference to the Spirit, except to affirm belief in him. In the continued battle with Arian notions of the Son's subordination to the Father as a creature made by God, courageous steps had to be taken in defining the relationships of the Persons within the Trinity towards each other, and whether they were created beings or not. It was thus the last quarter of the fourth century before the doctrine received something approaching a definitive expression. This developed understanding, which is part of the heritage of evangelicals and Orthodox alike as they seek to articulate 'the faith . . . once for all entrusted to the saints' (Jude 3), is summed up in the Nicene Creed: '. . . And [we believe] in the Holy Spirit, the Lord and life-giver, who proceeds from the Father, who with the Father and the Son together is worshipped and glorified, who spoke by the prophets.'

The chief architects of the developed doctrine of the Spirit were the Saints Gregory of Nazianzus, Gregory of Nyssa and Basil of Caesarea (the Cappadocian Fathers). Along with St Athanasius (c. 296–373), the Cappadocians defined the Spirit as *homoousion* ('of one and the same nature') with the Father and the Son. Basil's famous *Treatise on the Holy Spirit* was one of the greatest works on the Spirit in church history. What it did was to articulate the conviction of the early church's heart, that the Holy Spirit is no less than God Himself. Basil therefore rejected any notion that the Spirit was a created being: the Spirit was not merely a divinized creature, 'like God', but was of the same being as God.

From the New Testament Basil makes much of St Paul's assertion that 'the Lord is the Spirit, and where the Spirit of the Lord is, there is freedom' (2 Cor. 3:17). In that freedom Basil unlocks the keys of Scripture to reveal the Spirit not as power, supernatural influence, or sacred symbol, but as personal God. Whether we see the Spirit blowing wherever he chooses (Jn. 3:8), marking the Church with his seal (Eph. 1:13), or interceding on our behalf with groans which cannot be uttered (Rom. 8:26), or whether we turn to the Old Testament and read of God's Spirit breathing life into the dry bones of Israel (Ezek. 37:5–6), wherever we turn, Basil wrote, the Spirit is there. Even at the foundation of the world the Spirit broods and moves upon the waters (Gen. 1:2). The Spirit is intrinsically holy, worthy of the same glory, honour and adoration as the other Persons of the Godhead.[2]

Now the logic of all this, as Basil saw only too clearly, was that wherever the Father and the Son are, there is the Spirit also. This

Spirit is as much God as the Son is God. It therefore follows that the Spirit is also *homoousion* with the Father, as is the Son. Indeed the phrase the 'Spirit of God' used in the Septuagint version of the creation narrative of Genesis is Scripture's favourite name for the Spirit, who 'completes the all-praised and blessed Trinity'.[3] With great reserve,[4] and political acumen, Basil avoids calling the Spirit 'God' directly, but asserts his full divinity by insisting that he is not a creature.

But Basil did something else in his famous treatise of startling originality. He wanted to say of the Spirit that he was not only equal to God, Lord and life-giver, worthy of worship, of the same being as Father and Son, but that he, also like the Father and Son, existed as a distinct reality within the Godhead. Anxious to avoid the charges of tritheism, Basil adopted and adapted the word *hypostasis* for persons in the Godhead. Hitherto this had also been used as a synonym for *ousia* ('being') in the Christian tradition. All this meant that Basil was able on the one hand to assert that the Holy Spirit is 'indivisibly and inseparably joined to the Father and the Son',[5] and on the other hand to distinguish the distinct missions of the Persons of the Trinity.

As far as the divine economy, the mission in time of the Trinity, is concerned, there may be distinct functions but not separate actions of the divine Persons. There is no suggestion, for example, that Jesus came to establish the Church as a rock that would resist the onslaughts of hell, while the Spirit was out in the world missioning on his own, or operating a 'plan B' of salvation for all those in the world who for one reason or another will never enter the gates of the Church. There is no divided will in God, hence there can be no unilateral actions: where the Spirit is there is always the Son and Father. The idea that Son and Spirit are separate agents in the Godhead, with autonomous wills, is an absurdity. However, Basil suggests that while *separation* of Persons is foreign to the life of God, *distinction* can be made in the activities of the three Persons. God the Father, he claims, is the *original* cause of all things that are made; the *creative* cause is the Son, through whom all was made; and the *perfecting* cause is the Spirit.

## iii) The *Filioque* dispute

No East–West Christian dialogue can avoid the issue of the insertion of the *Filioque* clause into the Nicene Creed, because this clause remains, to this day, the only formal theological cause of the 'Great Schism' between Eastern and Western Christianity. Its significance derives at least in part from the fact that this has been the only creed to be universally accepted by East and West.

The text of the Nicene Creed says of the Spirit's origination that he 'proceeds from the Father'. This wording was based on the Gospel of John, which says that the Father will give the Paraclete (14:16) and that the Father will send the Holy Spirit (14:18). Most tellingly of all, Jesus speaks of 'the Counsellor . . . , whom I will send to you from the Father, the Spirit of truth who goes out ['proceeds' in Greek] from the Father' (15:26).

The idea that the Spirit can be said to proceed from the Father and the Son, rather than from the Father, first appeared in the West in the fourth century but it is the theology of Augustine of Hippo in the fifth century that put it on the map. It was in Spain, following a council at Toledo in 589, which inserted the clause into the Creed as an antidote to Arianism, that the *Filioque* was most prominent in the West. From there the *Filioque* spread to the Frankish empire, and under Charlemagne the Council of Frankfurt in 794 declared that the East was in error for not including it.

Although the Pope had expressed unhappiness at Charlemagne's actions, the *Filioque* issue flared up again in the 860s when East and West were competing for jurisdictional dominance in Bulgaria. Photius, Patriarch of Constantinople, argued vigorously against its insertion. On the one hand he made it clear that no see, including Rome, had the right to alter the creed without consent from all the churches. On the other hand he attacked the actual theology of the *Filioque* claiming that (a) it had no biblical authority, and that (b) by making the Father and the Son the 'cause' of the Spirit, the Spirit was now the only member of the Blessed Trinity that did not 'cause' or 'originate' another divine Person. Western theology was thus violating the belief that if a divine attribute was not a property of one particular Person, it was shared by all three. Following the

Greek Fathers, Photius believed that the Father alone was primary in the Trinity, not in the sense that he was ontologically superior (i.e. of a superior order of being), but that he was first among equals and the source of divinity. It was the Father who begot the Son, and from whom the Spirit proceeded. By altering that schema, and teaching that the Spirit proceeded from the Father and Son together, it was felt in the East that the West subordinated the Spirit to the Son and the Father; hence the Spirit became in effect the least member of the Trinity (although it must be pointed out that the late fifth-century Western Athanasian Creed, for example, makes clear the equality and co-eternity of the Spirit with the Father and the Son). The East also saw the Western doctrine as a threat to the position of the Father as the source of divinity within the Godhead. The view that the West is particularly weak in its doctrine of the Spirit as a result of the *Filioque* clause remains an Orthodox conviction to this day, although it is open to question, especially when presented in an extreme form which traces all Western theological and philosophical ills back to the insertion of this one word into the Nicene Creed.[6] Conversely, some Protestant writers hold that Orthodoxy has never given an adequate account of the relationship between the Son and the Spirit.

Throughout the eleventh century the *Filioque* was the theological symbol of the dispute about ecclesiastical authority. The East felt that the Bishop of Rome was trying to assert jurisdictional authority over the whole church, and that the unilateral decision to alter the Creed was the proof of Rome's imperial ambitions. Gradually the bad blood between Rome and Constantinople (the seat of the Eastern Roman Empire) spread to the other Eastern Churches of Jerusalem, Antioch and Alexandria. Any hope that schism could be avoided and the theological and jurisdictional problems resolved by peaceful means was dashed when in 1204 the Fourth Crusade chose to attack, sack and plunder Constantinople. Thousands were slaughtered, leaving a residue of great bitterness.

There was an attempt – politically motivated in the East by the threat of Islam – to resolve the dispute at the Council of Ferrara/Florence (1438–45). Despite the suggestion of a phrase to replace the *Filioque* – *per Filium* ('through the Son', an understanding which had appeared in Cappadocian thought) – and despite the fact that many Orthodox delegates to the Council accepted the doctrine contained therein, they were not able to convince the clergy and laity of the East to adopt it. In 1453 Byzantium fell to Islamic forces, and the Greek tradition was cut off from the West. Soon after, Rome had to deal with rebellion in its own ranks: with the advent of the Protestant Reformation, local matters took priority.

Protestants, including evangelicals, are seen by the Orthodox as having inherited the *Filioque* by default, as the Reformers received the Western version of the Nicene Creed from Rome. It has not often been a significant issue for evangelicals until Orthodox entry to the World Council of Churches stimulated ecumenical discussion about it, in part because of the evangelical tendency to sit more lightly to credal formulations and to emphasize spiritual experience. In terms of contemporary Orthodox-evangelical conversations, the Orthodox take the view that the *Filioque* is a Roman doctrine and not intrinsically Protestant or essential to Protestant thinking. They are thus perplexed as to why evangelicals do not reject it on biblical grounds, or charismatics on pneumatological ones. A number of Protestants (including evangelicals) who have examined the issues have concluded that the Orthodox viewpoint is closer to the teaching as well as the wording of Scripture. On the other hand, some have asserted that evangelical theology involves affirming the doctrine affirmed by the *Filioque* clause, which is that there is a certain equilibrium between the Father and the Son which runs through the whole economy of salvation. Whatever view evangelicals hold, achieving convergence on the *Filioque* issue is fundamental to the success of conversations with the Orthodox.[7] Discussion will need to focus not merely on the issue of who has the right to alter a universally accepted credal text, but on the scriptural evidence. It will also need to investigate the relationship between the Son and the Spirit, on which Orthodoxy lacks a pronouncement of comparable clarity to that concerning the relationship between the Father and the Spirit.

## iv) 'Everywhere present and filling all things': the Spirit in creation and providence

The Cappadocian Fathers believed that the Spirit was already active outside the Church through participation in creation. Evangelicals should have little problem with this, for Calvin asserted that 'it is the Spirit who, everywhere diffused, sustains all things, causes them to grow, and quickens them in heaven and earth'.[8] In the Nicene Creed, the Spirit is declared to be 'Lord and life-giver'; this role of the Spirit in initiating and sustaining creation is strongly attested by the Cappadocians. They believed that the non-Christian world, especially the Greek philosophers, could naturally discern something of God's presence.

Nevertheless, while they were eirenic towards the best aspects of their host culture, there was, in their minds, an absolute barrier to truth in antiquity, and that was the total absence of any sense of a terminus to history. The coming, and leaving of Jesus, through the Spirit's operation, initiates the beginning of the last days because Jesus shows us what the future of humankind will be by becoming incarnate on earth before history is ended. But it is the Spirit who makes this eschatological work possible. He does so in the Church not by making it an historical and material institution – that is the unique task of the incarnate Christ – but by making it a living eschatological community through adopting men and women to be the brothers and sisters of the risen and ascended Christ. It has been said that whereas Christ *institutes* the Church, it is the Spirit who *constitutes* it.

This same Spirit, who works to bring the Church to fulfilment, also perfects the divine will of the Father by working outside its visible boundaries – in the cosmos which, like humankind, also yearns to be free from the scars of sin (Rom. 8:22). Ultimately, therefore, the Spirit of the Church and the Lord of creation is the same God, and the redemptive task of the Spirit and his perfecting role in transfiguring creation and fallen culture are two aspects of the same work. For everywhere, and filling all things, the Spirit blows from the mouth of the Father in concert with the creative and sustaining power of the Word.

## v) The gifts of the Spirit

What of an issue which has so divided Evangelicalism in recent decades, the charismata? The charismatic experiences of the Orthodox saints, such as tears, visions, smells and light have something in common with contemporary claimed Pentecostal encounters with the Holy Spirit, although the latter generally lack the churchly context of the former. Similar criticisms of claims to such experiences have been made within each tradition: traditionalist Orthodox today accuse their charismatic brethren of emotionalism and *prelest* (pride leading to spiritual delusion), and similar criticisms were levelled at St Symeon the New Theologian, an important though neglected figure in the renewal of Orthodoxy. Stylianopoulos refers to Symeon as 'one of the greatest witnesses to the living presence of the Spirit in the Orthodox tradition'.[9] Symeon was but one of a number who reacted against this loss of the experience of the Spirit and the concomitant routinizing of spiritual life which seems to have emerged as an institutionalized church developed the characteristics that accompanied increasing power and influence in society. He insisted that experience of the power of the Spirit was for his own days, not just those of the apostles. Moreover, each person had to experience new birth, even those who had already received the Spirit in chrismation★. Regardless of status, all should receive baptism in the Spirit. Learning, theology, rank, title, position in an hierarchy – all meant nothing if the experience of the Spirit was absent.

Stylianopoulos sums up the effect that Symeon had:

> Symeon proved to be a prophetic voice in a Christian society inundated by formalism and ecclesiasticism. The incessant response to him was: but that's impossible! No one can live the apostolic life today! Pride is deluding you! Symeon was also persecuted by monks and hierarchs. He was finally driven into exile. I cannot think of a more telling example of a Christian tradition which, despite its rejection of the *filioque* and its correct teaching about the Holy Spirit, nevertheless was marked by such clericalism and formalism that actual readiness to welcome the presence of the Spirit in the practical life of the Church was the exception rather than the rule.[10]

More recently, the Charismatic movement, with its stress on the gifts of the Spirit as available to all and its expectation of the supernatural, has permeated much of English Evangelicalism. Yet the movement often misses some of the deeper issues arising from a consideration of the Spirit's work, and contemporary evangelicals tend to lack depth in their understanding of his activity in the Church or the world, limiting it to his work in the individual.

## vi) The Holy Spirit in evangelical thought

Evangelicals, especially those of Reformed convictions, have provided detailed expositions of the work of the Spirit in individual conversion. More recently, under the influence of the Charismatic movement, evangelicals have tended to focus on the gifts of the Spirit. However, from a historical perspective there is much more to be said concerning evangelical pneumatology.

Calvin has been characterized as the 'theologian of the Holy Spirit'.[11] For him, the Spirit unites us by faith with Christ in heaven: it is the Spirit who ensures the effectiveness of the sacraments as signs and seals of grace, and who is the agent of the inner transformation of believers though their union with Christ. Calvin was concerned not merely with theoretical definition of the Holy Spirit, but with appropriating his ministries as described in Scripture.[12]

Some sixteenth-century radicals foreshadowed many modern charismatic emphases, and Anabaptist thinking and church practice has proved increasingly attractive to some evangelicals in recent decades as they struggle to come to terms with a 'post-Christian' society. The Anabaptists (so called from their insistence on re-baptizing as believers those who had been baptized as infants) allowed all to contribute in worship and study of the Scriptures, and their approach to interpreting Scripture arguably gave greater place to the illuminating role of the Spirit than did that of the mainline Reformers. For the Anabaptists, the Spirit was seen as being at work in the lives of believers, enlightening them, illuminating the Scriptures to them, and transforming their lives inwardly. He produced real change, which was observable in the commitment to a life of discipleship, understood as following Christ in bearing the cross and giving oneself in service for others, especially fellow members of the body of believers. However, some less orthodox radicals, such as Caspar Schwenckfeld (1490–1561), foreshadowed some modern evangelicals and charismatics in a weak ecclesiology and a belief that the activity of the Spirit in the individual's life rendered outward sacraments, and sometimes even outward worship, unnecessary (as did the later Quakers, a group who sprang from the Puritan tradition).

Seventeenth-century Puritans produced extensive typologies of the Spirit's work in the soul which were closely linked with their understanding of the order of the different aspects of salvation, and gained a reputation as wise pastors. In the process, they immersed themselves in the Fathers (as was the norm in their day), some referring to them more than to the Reformers.[13] Richard Sibbes and John Owen produced the largest body of literature on the Holy Spirit in Anglo-American theology.[14] The Puritan conception of the Christian life, with its emphasis on perseverance, is given flesh in the Baptist John Bunyan's hero, Christian, in his classic *Pilgrim's Progress*.

For the Puritans, working out a detailed theology went hand-in-hand with a deep personal experience of the Spirit's touch. Although they limited the extraordinary *charismata* in the New Testament to the apostolic age, they taught that believers could be inwardly assured of their regenerate status. The *Westminster Confession* (1646) stated that such assurance was founded upon the divine truth of the scriptural promises of salvation, evidence within the believer's life of God's grace at work (demonstrating that they were indeed heirs to the promises) and the inward testimony of the Spirit bearing witness to the believer's status as a child of God.[15]

On the Continent, the Pietists reacted against the perceived dryness of orthodox Lutheranism with a renewed stress on vital personal religion.[16] Like the Anabaptists, they believed that the Spirit alone could give such life, apart from which the sacraments of the Church, or orthodox belief, were valueless.

While the Puritans saw complete sanctification as something only attained at death, John Wesley thought it could be obtained in this life. Deeply influenced by the Desert Fathers (Egyptian monks of the fourth century), he was very close to Orthodox teaching in his understanding of how the Holy Spirit operates in activating the conscience and enabling repentance.[17] For him, sanctification or 'Christian perfection' was the goal of the Christian life, and he understood it in a way which ran parallel to the monastic tradition of perfect love for God and neighbour. In such an understanding, perfection comes as the Spirit gives power, resulting in the fruits of love, joy, peace – but not in such a way that human effort is excluded. In this synergism* we again find contact with the monastic Orthodox tradition. Here are echoes of *theosis*. In both there is a fusing of divine and human energies in a continued act of repentance. Christian living is not simply a selfish working out of salvation for oneself, but of genuine concern to serve the other.

Nearer to the present, the Pentecostal movement has recovered the experiential aspect of pneumatology, as adherents have reflected on what the Spirit has done in their lives. An experiential approach to doctrinal formulation may need to be employed with caution but it is undoubtedly present in the New Testament, for it was as believers reflected on what they had seen and heard of Christ that they came to a new awareness of who he was and an enriched understanding of the scriptural prophecies.

Evangelicals today would assent to the biblical teaching outlined above concerning the Holy Spirit. Although relatively few would be familiar with patristic thinking, most of it would probably be seen as unexceptionable. Evangelical pneumatology has tended to be stronger on the Spirit's work in individuals than on his work in the Church (perhaps evangelicals have lost sight of some of their heritage in this respect), and the former is where it has a distinctive contribution to make. Contemporary British evangelical thought concerning the Spirit may be outlined by taking each of the adjectives used in the Evangelical Alliance's Doctrinal Basis, which describes the Spirit's work as 'illuminating, regenerating, indwelling and sanctifying'.

It is the Spirit who illuminates the understanding, enabling individuals to grasp the significance of the biblical message (cf. Jn. 14:26, 16:13; 1 Cor. 2:10); more than that, the Spirit works to convince them that this is a message addressed directly to them, which describes their spiritual state, and to which they must respond (Jn. 16:8–11; 1 Thes. 1:5).

Regeneration is a term used in contemporary evangelical thinking to refer to the Spirit's work in making people spiritually alive, hence the frequent evangelical description of Christians as those who have been 'born again' (Jn. 3:1–8). The Holy Spirit unites them with Christ in a personal relationship through faith, so that they receive the benefits which he gained for them by his death and resurrection. All those thus united with Christ are, by virtue of this union, constituted members of his body, the Church (1 Cor. 12:13; see Ch. 7).

Evangelicals have always been known for their stress on the idea of Christianity as a personal relationship with God. It is the Spirit indwelling believers who assures them of their standing as children of God through Christ. Objectively, he convinces them of the divine origin and truthfulness of Holy Scripture; subjectively, he grants them peace concerning their acceptance with God and a persuasion that Christ's death and resurrection have availed to save them personally, so that they are enabled to call God 'Father' (Rom. 8:15; Gal. 4:6). It is also the Spirit who gifts each believer as a member of the body of Christ, enabling them to serve God, one another and the society in which they live (1 Cor. 12:7–11; 1 Pet. 4:10).

Conversion to Christ is only a beginning: sanctification, or transformation into the likeness of Christ, is a lifelong process in which the Spirit is at work to produce his fruit in believers (Gal. 5:22–3). They are not passive in this, but are called to persevere, to 'keep in step with the Spirit' (Gal. 5:25).[18]

## vii) Summary

*Theosis* may be seen as the Orthodox analogue for Western formulations of spiritual rebirth and renewal.[19] Whether they use the terminology of *theosis*, sanctification or perseverance, both traditions agree in seeing God at work *in* as well as *for* the believer through the power of the Holy Spirit. It is the Spirit, the Giver of life, who mediates the presence of the risen Christ. Differences in expression may in part be semantic, and the areas of practical agreement be greater than is at first apparent. The pneumatologies of both sides were forged in the fire of personal experience and are worthy of hard study just as they call for hard work.

## Notes

1 J. I. Packer, *Keep in Step with the Spirit* (Leicester: IVP, 1984), p. 66.

2 Cf. Stanley M. Burgess and Gary B. McGee (eds), *Dictionary of Pentecostal and Charismatic Movements* (Grand Rapids, MI: Zondervan, 1988), p. 425.

3 St Basil, *On the Holy Spirit*, §45.

4 J. N. D. Kelly, *Early Christian Doctrines* (London: A. & C. Black, 1976), p. 260.

5 St Basil, *On the Holy Spirit*, §37.

6 For a lucid and not uncritical exposition of Orthodox objections to the *Filioque* clause, see Kallistos Ware, *The Orthodox Church* (Harmondsworth: Pelican, 1997), pp. 210–18.

7 A wide-ranging survey of the historical, exegetical and doctrinal issues associated with the *Filioque* clause is provided by Gerald Bray in his article 'The *Filioque* clause in history and theology', *Tyndale Bulletin* 34 (1983), pp. 91–145. Especially noteworthy is his discussion of the parallels between the thought of St Gregory Palamas and John Calvin, both of whom devoted considerable space to discussion of the work of the Holy Spirit in the believer.

8 John Calvin, *Institutes of the Christian Religion*, 1.13.14; ed. J. T. McNeill, tr. F. L. Battles (Philadelphia, PA: Westminster/London: SCM, 1960), vol. I, p. 138.

9 Theodore Stylianopoulos, 'The *Filioque*: Dogma, *theologoumenon* or error?', in Theodore Stylianopoulos and S. M. Heim (eds), *Spirit of Truth: Ecumenical Perspectives on the Holy Spirit* (Brookline, MA: Holy Cross Orthodox Press, 1986), p. 56.

10 Ibid., pp. 56–7.

11 A. P. F. Sell, *The Great Debate: Calvinism, Arminianism and Salvation* (Worthing: H. E. Walter, 1982), p. 3.

12  R. Lovelace, 'Pneumatological issues in American Presbyterianism', in Stylianopoulos and Heim, p. 111.

13  Ibid., p. 112.

14  Ibid., p. 113. Owen produced *Pneumatologia; Of Communion With God the Father, Son and Holy Ghost; A Discourse of the Work of the Holy Spirit in Prayer;* and *The Grace and Duty of Being Spiritually-Minded.*

15  *Westminster Confession*, 18.2; in John H. Leith (ed.), *Creeds of the Churches* (Atlanta: John Knox, 1973), p. 213.

16  A useful introduction to the renewed stress on experience evident in some of the seventeenth- and eighteenth-century groups covered in this section (and others, such as Orthodoxy and Judaism) is Ted A. Campbell, *The Religion of the Heart* (Columbia, SC: University of Carolina Press, 1992).

17  Roberta Bondi, 'The role of the Holy Spirit from a United Methodist Perspective', in Stylianopoulos and Heim, p. 124. Two studies of the relationship of Wesley's thought with that of Eastern Christianity are Ted A. Campbell, *John Wesley and Christian Antiquity* (Nashville, TN: Kingswood Books, 1991); and Randy L. Maddox, *Responsible Grace: John Wesley's Practical Theology* (Nashville, TN: Abingdon, 1994).

18  A helpful overview of evangelical thinking about the Spirit and Christian experience is provided in Bruce Milne, *Know the Truth* (Leicester: IVP, 1980), part 5.

19  Lovelace, in Stylianopoulos and Heim, p. 106.

# 7

# The Church

## i) Common ground

When one reads an evangelical or an Orthodox exposition of the nature of the Church, one will find many things that both groups believe, especially regarding the Trinitarian, Christological and pneumatological ground of the Church – to use Kallistos Ware's categories.[1] Probably few evangelical or Orthodox theologians would dissent from the following summary:

> The Church has its origin in the Person and work of Christ. By virtue of his incarnation, death and resurrection, he has inaugurated a new humanity which is a saving transformation of the old apostate humanity in Adam. The Holy Spirit, poured out at Pentecost, forms this new humanity as the mystical body of Christ, communicating his risen life to all who believe in him. The resulting community, having access to the Father through union with Christ in the Spirit, reflects the being of the Trinity by manifesting a fellowship of persons in a shared life. The Church is the centre of God's purposes [evangelical 'dispensationalists'* would disagree here], the locus of his restoring work in creation, and destined to inherit the cosmos when Christ returns.

Alongside these similarities, Evangelicalism and Orthodoxy reveal significant differences in the way they make use of their common ground. What follows is an outline of the *distinctive* evangelical and Orthodox approaches to the Church (for evangelical attitudes towards the Orthodox Church, see Ch. 11).

## ii) The evangelical approach

### a) The foundational concept: the Church universal

Foundational to evangelical concepts of the Church is the belief that *the Church is the community or society of all those who through faith are united to Christ through the indwelling Holy Spirit.* Sometimes evangelicals see this community as including the glorified spirits of believers in heaven. More often the focus is more specifically on that part of the Church which is on earth – the total number of true believers in the world. It is in this sense that evangelicals would describe the Church as 'catholic'.

This definition of the Church is logically and theologically foundational, and gathers into itself several important evangelical convictions:

1. The Church is essentially *people*, not buildings or institutions.
2. The Church is composed of *those who are united to Christ by faith*. Some paedobaptists would also see the children of believers as belonging to the Church.
3. Although credal orthodoxy (right belief) can exist without living faith, most evangelicals would insist that living faith cannot exist without credal orthodoxy, at least in some basic form. 'Faith' (personal) is rooted in 'the faith' (objective). Thus if the Church is those who are united to Christ by faith, it is by that very token a people whose faith involves a basic credal orthodoxy – *those who confess the faith*, sometimes defined in terms of the early creeds or later Protestant confessions, but more often in terms of certain fundamental doctrines to which believers are expected to assent.
4. The Church is *a people indwelt by the Holy Spirit*. It is the Spirit who regenerates sinners, unites them to Christ, gives them faith, sanctifies them, and thereby constitutes and sustains them as Christ's believing people. For most evangelicals, this is allied with a deep suspicion of any ecclesiology which puts institutions and structures (or even sacraments) in the foreground (some appeal to texts such as 2 Tim. 3:5). They thus

face serious criticism from the Orthodox (and from some
fellow evangelicals) because of their apparent devaluing of
baptism as a rite of initiation into the people of God.

Another central evangelical conviction about the nature of the
Church is *the priesthood of all believers* (cf. 1 Pet. 2:9). This means that
all Christians – all who are united to Christ through faith – are
constituted priests in him by virtue of their faith and baptism. This
is understood in terms of enjoying direct access to God through
Christ.

### b) The Church visible and invisible

Because historic Evangelicalism has held to such a concept of the
Church, it means that the Church of Jesus Christ is, first and
foremost, to be understood as an 'invisible church'. This was a major
flash-point in the controversies of the Reformation era, and also
figures prominently in Orthodox critiques of Evangelicalism.

It is true that the concept of the 'invisible church' can be and has
been abused by evangelicals to justify contempt for existing
denominations and for committed membership in local
congregations, and to gloss over the scandal of division. Some
consider that it is so susceptible to misunderstanding as to be
unhelpful and misleading. However, abuse does not destroy proper
use. Most evangelicals would still affirm a true and important sense
in which the true church on earth is 'invisible'.

The *visible* universal Church of *professing* believers is a mixture of
wheat and tares. No human beings are competent to pronounce
infallibly or with certainty which person belongs to which category,
however hard they might try. Man looks on the outward
appearance, but God alone sees the heart (1 Sam. 16:7). Therefore
only God can see infallibly who the true believers are (2 Tim. 2:19).
Furthermore, the Church, in evangelical thinking, consists *essentially*
in this company of true believers, to which merely 'nominal'
believers (those who profess faith outwardly but lack faith inwardly)
do not belong. There is therefore an inevitable contrast between the
Church as *God* sees it – the total number of the Spirit-indwelt

faithful in Christ – and the church as *man* sees it – the company of outwardly professing believers. This is what historic Protestantism and Evangelicalism mean by the 'invisible' and 'visible' church.[2]

For historic Evangelicalism, the invisible church and the visible church are not two separate entities: rather, they overlap with one another. However, the extent to which they overlap is the subject of divergent opinions within evangelical ecclesiology. Traditions such as the Baptists, stressing the idea of the 'gathered' or 'pure' church made up of those who join by baptism upon profession of personal faith, seek to make that overlap as large as possible, both by excluding those whom they do not recognize as believers and, increasingly, also by including all those whom they do recognize as believers (even if not baptized). Others, such as Anglicans, Lutherans and many of the Reformed, would espouse a 'mixed' concept of the Church on earth, in which unbelievers as well as believers are a part; they have often also held a 'territorial' understanding of ecclesiology, in which the visible church comprises all those born and baptized in a particular territory.

## c) The local church

All this leads us to the other crucial use of the term 'church' by evangelicals, which is the local church – the gathered congregation or assembly of professing believers. What is the relationship between the universal Church and the local church? There are differences of opinion among evangelicals here, reflecting divergent under-standings of church government. However, in a general sense, the universal Church is made manifest in local churches; they are the universal Church taking on concrete form in specific places. Classical Protestantism offered two identity-marks of a true church: 'Wherever we see the Word of God purely preached and heard, and the sacraments administered according to Christ's institution, there, it is not to be doubted, a church of God exists.'[3]

What generalizations can be made about Evangelicalism's concept of the local church which will be of special relevance to the Orthodox?

1. The evangelical concept of 'ministry' differs from that of Orthodoxy. Evangelicals understand apostolic succession fundamentally in terms of *standing in the stream of apostolic teaching*: he succeeds the apostles who teaches what the apostles taught. The Orthodox would also acknowledge the idea of doctrinal succession but would see it as guaranteed by a visible succession of bishops in a given diocese (see Ch. 2 and Section 4 below).

2. Historically, evangelicals have given a high place to preaching in their concept of the ministry and local church life. This is connected with the evangelical view of Scripture's supreme authority as God's written word.

3. Evangelical church buildings have no sacred spaces where only certain authorized persons are allowed to tread. Architecturally, if any part of the building's interior dominates it will be the pulpit.

### iii) The Orthodox approach

#### a) The centrality of the Church

Perhaps the first thing that strikes an evangelical is how large the Church looms in Orthodox thinking and piety. Ecclesiology occupies the fundamental place in Orthodox thought which is occupied by the doctrine of salvation in evangelical thought. Furthermore, when evangelicals think about salvation, they think about the individual's relationship with Christ through personal faith, but when Orthodox think about salvation, they are more likely to think first (though not exclusively) of the Church – even to say that 'salvation is the Church'. By that they mean the Orthodox Church. Kallistos Ware sums it up like this: 'The word "Orthodoxy" has the double meaning of "right belief" and "right glory" (or "right worship"). The Orthodox, therefore . . . regard their Church as the Church which guards and teaches the true belief about God and which glorifies Him with right worship, that is, *as nothing less than the Church of Christ on earth*.'[4]

## b) Orthodoxy as the true church

A crucial aspect of Orthodoxy is stated clearly by Archbishop Paul of Finland: 'the Eastern Orthodox Church is organically the same congregation or *ecclesia* which was born at the outpouring of the Holy Spirit in Jerusalem at Pentecost'.[5] For Orthodox believers, there is a direct and unbroken spiritual, theological and institutional continuity between their church now and the first-century church in Jerusalem. Therefore 'here on earth there is a single, visible community which alone can claim to be the one true Church'[6] – Orthodoxy. For the Orthodox, their community is no denomination; it is quite simply the Church of Christ – the same church that the apostles founded. This conviction gives rise to a strong feeling of history and antiquity to the Orthodox believer's church-consciousness. Indeed, this is one of the most attractive things about Orthodoxy for evangelicals who convert to it. A recurrent phenomenon within Evangelicalism has been that of groups seeking to replicate 'the New Testament church', notable examples being the Brethren and Pentecostal movements; some have satisfied this longing by joining what they see as the present continuation of 'New Testament Christianity' – Orthodoxy.

There is, admittedly, a strand within Evangelicalism which puts a high value on historical continuity, as indeed the Reformers themselves did. The difference is that evangelicals would not see this continuity as being essentially tied to institutional, clerical and liturgical forms, but as a continuity of faith. The evangelical heroes of the Middle Ages – the Waldensians, Lollards and Hussites – ended up outside the historic institutional structures of medieval church life. Many evangelicals have argued that the truest apostolic continuity lay with such groups, because they preserved more fully and purely the apostolic faith. This would be an outworking of the widespread evangelical belief that the people of God in every age are the faithful remnant rather than the mass belonging to a visible institution.

Jesus' prayer for the oneness of believers in Jn. 17:20–23 provides an important crux for Orthodox-evangelical debate. The unity among his people for which Jesus prays must be a visible unity, if its effect is that the world will believe (v.21), and know that the Father sent the Son and has loved the disciples with the love with which he has loved the Son (v.23). Orthodox will be inclined to locate this visible unity in what the world can see of a united Orthodox Church. By contrast, they will point to the visible disunity among evangelicals – the multiplicity of denominations – as evidence that Evangelicalism here fails to fulfil Christ's intentions. An evangelical response might be that Orthodoxy does not necessarily look so united as Orthodox claim, divided along ethnic-jurisdictional lines even where the ethnic groups are all found in a common land speaking a common language (e.g. in the United States). Other Orthodox disunities come to mind, such as those between Old Calendarists and New Calendarists, or between the Moscow Patriarchate and the Russian Orthodox Church Abroad. This kind of debate can easily degenerate into an unedifying spectacle of 'who is the greatest sinner'. Perhaps it would be more fruitful to examine afresh the nature of the visible unity that Christ had in mind in these verses. Since it is asserted to rest on the kind of visible unity seen to be enjoyed by the Father and the Son, it may be that Christ's intention is to point to a unity of love, rather than an organizational unity: 'All men will know that you are my disciples if you love one another' (Jn. 13:35). Of course, this interpretation might prove equally contentious.

## c) Definitions

### A. The Church – divine and human

As with Christology, Orthodox ecclesiology speaks of the Church as being both divine and human, a somewhat different polarity from the visible/invisible one often used by evangelicals. The Church is a divine institution, animated by the Holy Spirit who constitutes it as the Body of Christ; grafted into Christ by the Spirit through baptism, chrismation and the Eucharist, believers live in Christ and enjoy communion with the Father, experiencing a foretaste of the life of the age to come. Yet the Church is also a human institution, marked by human failings. In its human aspect, the Church is as yet imperfect, but in its divine aspect, the Church is a vast and glorious entity which calls forth our reverence and respect. Such a conception of the Church is unfamiliar to many evangelicals, although they may readily recognize that the New Testament provides the raw material for it; Calvin, too, spoke in a similar way in formulating his understanding of the visible and invisible church.

### B. The Church as the community of those who believe in Christ

In Orthodoxy there is a stress on the whole body of the faithful, laity as well as clergy, as constituting the Church. However, there are still important differences between Orthodoxy and Evangelicalism in their concept of church-as-believers. For a start, the content of what is believed would differ. As the modern Greek theologian Athanasios Frangopoulos says, the believing church means 'those who share the same faith and confession, the true, i.e. the Orthodox faith'.[7] However, Orthodoxy would define the faith rather differently from Evangelicalism in significant aspects, such as its understanding of apostolic succession, the sacraments, Mariology, icons, invocation of saints and its dominant model of soteriology as deification. So while Orthodoxy does conceive of the Church as 'the community of all believers', this does not *necessarily* mean that it recognizes evangelicals as among those believers of whom the community is composed.

### C. The Church as a worshipping community

Orthodoxy has historically seen its form of worship – the Liturgy – as lying at its heart. The status thus accorded to Orthodox worship makes it almost a co-equal partner with the Bible as a channel of revealed truth. In fact, the Liturgy could be understood as a comprehensive manifestation of heavenly realities – 'the earthly heaven'.[8] And so in Orthodoxy, the Church itself, as 'incarnated' in its worship, is a sort of vast living icon of heaven, which initiates worshippers into spiritual reality. Necessarily, then, those who do not participate in Orthodox worship are partially or even totally cut off from the 'place' where God unites himself with human beings.

At one level evangelicals would agree in defining the Church as a worshipping community, that the Trinity is the object of worship, and that to worship the Trinity wrongly is not a good thing. However, most would tend to have a relatively tolerant attitude to forms of worship. Evangelicals would see a church's forms of worship as being subject to the distorting effects of sin and the relativizing effects of history and culture, and therefore decisively *under* the critical authority of Scripture, which alone is infallible. Forms of worship are thus always open to question, correction and revision in the light of Scripture.

### D. The Church as an apostolic and sacramental community

The 'mysteries' is the Orthodox term for what most other Christians would call 'sacraments' or 'ordinances'. For Orthodoxy, the Spirit communicates the risen life of Christ not through *any* sacraments, but through *Orthodox* sacraments. There is a strong tradition within Evangelicalism which would conceive of the sacraments as instrumentally life-giving in the Spirit's hands, but which would not tie this to any specially empowered priestly order. For Orthodoxy, however, the clergy are such an order, through their *apostolic succession* – the apostles laid hands on the first bishops, those bishops laid hands on their successors, and so forth (although they are also regarded as part of the people). As one bishop is consecrated to succeed another, the deposit of the faith and the commission to shepherd the flock in the power of the Holy Spirit is handed on (cf. Ch. 2). Evangelicals have tended to regard apostolic succession as a matter of continuing faithfulness to apostolic doctrine, but the Orthodox see faithful teaching as channelled through an apostolic succession of bishops.

Orthodoxy holds that it is impossible to speak of the Church without speaking of the role of the bishop. This is because, by virtue of the operation of the Holy Spirit, the bishop is the 'fountain of all the Mysteries . . . through which we obtain salvation'.[9] It is argued that such a view has very early roots, in the teaching of St Ignatius of Antioch (see Ch. 2). There is a sort of logical chain: *bishop-sacraments-salvation*. Evangelicals need to understand the view of the sacraments that Orthodoxy holds. It is not apostolic succession, nor the words of consecration spoken by the priest, but the activity of the Spirit that makes the sacraments effective. In baptism, the believer receives the Spirit inwardly and so is incorporated spiritually and redemptively into Christ; in the Eucharist, Christ through the agency of the Spirit causes his body and blood to dwell in the communicant to effect his deification. Nonetheless, priests are the only means whereby these life-giving sacraments can take place. It therefore seems to follow that there can be no life-giving sacraments apart from a priesthood rooted in apostolic succession. For mainstream Orthodoxy, ever since the East-West schism, this priesthood has effectively been found only in the Orthodox Church, which is the only truly apostolic and sacramental community. Protestant churches are thus no churches, their sacraments are no sacraments, and the Spirit is not received through them. However, a less 'exclusivist' school of thought in Orthodoxy has been willing to see God's grace conveyed in some meaningful sense through non-Orthodox sacraments as an 'uncovenanted mercy' from God (see Section 4 below).

## E. The Church as infallible

According to Kallistos Ware, 'Christ and the Holy Spirit cannot err, and since the Church is Christ's body, since it is a continued Pentecost, it is therefore infallible.' He expands on this with a quotation from Dositheus, the seventeenth-century Patriarch of Jerusalem: 'it is impossible for the Catholic [i.e. Orthodox] Church to err, or to be at all deceived, or ever to choose falsehood instead of truth'.[10] To an evangelical, this sounds rather like Roman Catholic teaching about the Church. The momentous difference is that in Catholicism this infallibility in defining divinely revealed doctrine is lodged primarily in the papacy and secondarily in the body of bishops gathered under the Pope to exercise their teaching office in certain defined circumstances,[11] whereas in Orthodoxy it is expressed through the life of the whole Church, for example in the doctrinal definitions of the Ecumenical Councils. The Orthodox view of infallibility is seen as being more collective than that of Rome, and less authoritarian or clerical: there is a certain 'fuzziness' about it which saves it from becoming mechanistic. A Russian term for the Orthodox approach to the question of authority is *sobornost**. Many Orthodox theologians would argue that the Ecumenical Councils were infallible not merely because the bishops got together and promulgated a creed, but because those creeds were then received by the whole Church as orthodox – as testifying to apostolic truth, recognized as such by the whole body of the faithful.

For evangelical ecclesiology, this raises two significant issues. Many evangelical theologians would accept the doctrinal *content* of what the first four, or even the first six, Ecumenical Councils decreed.[12] Yet they, like the sixteenth-century Reformers, would not accept the decrees of the Ecumenical Councils as *infallible* because received by the whole Church at the time, but as *true* because in harmony with Scripture.

### F. The Church as the community of the living and the dead

Finally, another important aspect of Orthodox ecclesiology is its belief in the oneness of the church on earth with the church in heaven. This finds particular expression in prayer: the church on earth prays for the souls of the departed, and the church in heaven prays for the pilgrims on earth. The belief that the saints in heaven pray for believers on earth forms the basis for the invocation of saints – asking the glorified saints to pray for us, just as we would ask fellow-believers on earth to pray for us. This in turn links with *icons* of the saints, which manifest their heavenly reality to believers. Bulgakov sums up the Orthodox view:

> The Saints are our intercessors and our protectors in the heavens and, in consequence, living and active members of the Church militant. Their blessed presence in the Church manifests itself in their pictures and their relics. They surround us with a cloud of prayer, a cloud of the glory of God. This cloud of witnesses does not separate us from Christ, but brings us nearer, unites us to Him. The Saints are not mediators between God and man – this would set aside the Unique Mediator, which is Christ – but they are our friends, who pray for us, and aid us in our Christian ministry and in our communion with Christ.[13]

Chief among these heavenly intercessors is the Virgin Mary: 'the Virgin remains the mother of the human race for which she prays and intercedes. This is why the Church addresses to her its supplications, invoking her aid.'[14]

Historic evangelical ecclesiology acknowledges the spiritual oneness of the church on earth and in heaven; evangelicals would agree with Orthodox that all form part of the one body of Christ.

Further, representative evangelicals have been quite willing to admit that in a general sense, the church in heaven prays for the church on earth. In Calvin's words, 'In asserting the intercession of the saints, if all you mean is that they continually pray for the completion of Christ's kingdom, on which the salvation of all the faithful depends, there is none of us who calls it in question.'[15] However, evangelicals have not been willing to go beyond this and address invocations to the glorified saints, for three reasons:

1. 'reverent agnosticism' – there is no way of actually knowing that particular saints can eavesdrop on our particular prayers;
2. there is no warrant in Scripture for invoking the departed;
3. in practice it leads easily to superstition as people put their hope in the intercession of saints rather than that of Christ.

### iv) Ecclesiology and salvation

Orthodox ecclesiology might seem so exclusive that it offers nothing to evangelicals but 'Come and join us or remain cut off from grace.' Some, indeed, would say precisely that. They regard the renewal of Orthodoxy as involving the cessation of ecumenical involvement, ecumenism being seen as a by-word for compromise.[16] However, the issues are somewhat more complex, as Russian bishops have recently acknowledged.[17] There appear to be three main approaches among the Orthodox to the status of evangelicals as believers, and hence to evangelical churches:

1. There is *no* salvation outside Orthodoxy, therefore evangelicals are not our brothers in Christ. Evangelical churches are mere human organizations, and the Spirit does not work in and through their ministries and sacraments.

2. There *may* be salvation outside Orthodoxy, and the Spirit may be at work in and through evangelical churches, because God is merciful. But no Orthodox can presume to say whether an evangelical should be accepted as a brother in Christ. Only God knows.

3. There *is* salvation outside Orthodoxy, and the Orthodox should recognize evangelicals as brothers in Christ. But the *fullness* of

Christianity is found only in Orthodoxy.[18] Those with this perspective would be willing to grant that evangelical churches possess some of the characteristics of the Church, but it would be rare to find an Orthodox who would consider evangelical churches to be as fully 'church' as the Orthodox churches.

There is no real evangelical counterpart to this debate, apart from that which began in the Reformation era concerning whether the Roman Catholic Church should be regarded as truly a Christian church. Evangelicals do not fuse together so closely an individual's salvation with membership of an ecclesiastical body; the fundamental evangelical question is always, 'Does the individual believe and trust in Jesus Christ for salvation?' If so, that individual belongs to the church as God sees it, to whatever ecclesiastical body he or she professes allegiance. Evangelicals with no axe to grind would have a natural bias to believing and hoping that there are many within Orthodoxy who belong to the church of true believers. Such a perspective could, if reflected upon carefully, have considerable implications for evangelical mission practice in Orthodox areas (see Ch. 11).

## Notes

1 Kallistos Ware, *The Orthodox Church* (Harmondsworth: Pelican, 1997), p. 240.

2 See, for example, John Calvin, *Institutes of the Christian Religion*, 4.1.7; ed. J. T. McNeill, tr. F. L. Battles (Philadelphia, PA: Westminster/London: SCM, 1960), vol. II, pp. 1021–2.

3 Calvin, *Institutes*, 4.1.9; vol II, p. 1023.

4 Ware, *Church*, p. 8.

5 Archbishop Paul of Finland, *The Faith We Hold* (Crestwood, NY: St Vladimir's Seminary Press, 1980), p. 15.

6 Ware, *Church*, p. 245.

7 Athanasios Frangopoulos, *Our Orthodox Christian Faith* (Athens: The Brotherhood of Theologians, 1996[7]), p. 186.

8 Ware, *Church*, p. 264.

9 'Confession of Dositheus', Decree 10, in John H. Leith (ed.), *Creeds of the Churches* (Atlanta: John Knox, 1973), p. 493.

10  Ware, *Church*, p. 248, quoting the 'Confession of Dositheus', Decree 12.

11  *The Catechism of the Catholic Church* (London: Geoffrey Chapman, 1994), §§890-1, pp. 206–7.

12  Cf. the Reformed thologian Charles Hodge (1797–1878), in his 'Open Letter to Pope Pius IX', reprinted in *Banner of Truth* 415 (April 1988), pp. 22–5.

13  Sergius Bulgakov, *The Orthodox Church* (Crestwood, NY: St Vladimir's Seminary Press, 1988), p. 119.

14  Ibid., p. 118.

15  John Calvin, 'Reply to Sadoleto', in Henry Beveridge and Jules Bonnet (eds), *Tracts and Letters* (Edinburgh: Calvin Translation Society, 1844), vol. 1, p. 110.

16  Orthodox attitudes to ecumenism are complex, and are shaped not only by theological concerns but also by a range of external factors which include nationalist aspirations, political pressure, dependence on Western financial assistance and the influence of pluralist and democratic ideas. As with Evangelicalism, there is a spectrum of opinion ranging from total rejection of all forms of ecumenical contact through to enthusiastic co-operation in ecumenical (and, in the case of Orthodoxy, even inter-faith) activities. For fuller discussion of the factors influencing Orthodox views on ecumenism, see the articles in *Religion, State & Society* 26.2 (June 1998).

From a historical perspective, it is important to note that the Orthodox have been involved in the modern ecumenical movement since its inception: in 1920, the Patriarch of Constantinople sent an encyclical letter to all Christian churches calling for closer inter-church co-operation. For the text of this, see Gennadios Limouris (ed.), *Orthodox Visions of Eucmenism: Statements, Messages and Reports on the Ecumenical Movement 1902–1992* (Geneva: World Council of Churches, 1994), pp. 9–11.

17  'Basic Principles of the Attitude of the Russian Orthodox Church toward the other Christian Confessions' (a statement adopted by the Jubilee Bishops' Council of the Russian Orthodox Church on 14 August 2000).

18  This may be compared with modern Roman Catholic thinking concerning the status of Protestant churches; see the Dogmatic Constitution *Lumen Gentium*, §§14–5, in Austin Flannery (ed.), *Vatican Council II: The Conciliar and Post-Conciliar Documents* (Leominster: Fowler Wright, 1975), pp. 366–7.

# 8

# Scripture and Tradition

Orthodox and evangelicals share a high view of Scripture. This fact has often been forgotten or undervalued, partly because Orthodoxy assigns great importance to Tradition and partly because, unlike Evangelicalism, it has not had to devote so much energy to defending the divine origin and authority of Scripture against theological liberalism and reductionist biblical critics. Thus an exalted regard for the Bible has never been a distinctive badge of Orthodoxy, as it has of Evangelicalism.

## i) The doctrine of Scripture

Although it would be a mistake to assume that Orthodoxy operates with as systematic a doctrine of Scripture as many evangelicals do, Orthodoxy's high view of Scripture may be illustrated from the *Catechism* of the Russian theologian, St Philaret (1782–1867), who was Metropolitan of Moscow and an influential teacher and leader in church and state. Although Philaret cannot be regarded as fully representative of Orthodox belief in every age and region (no individual Orthodox can ever be so regarded), his *Catechism* remains one of Orthodoxy's weightiest doctrinal statements, having been adopted by the Russian Church in 1839.[1] Philaret was recently canonized, and his writings are warmly commended by Georges Florovsky (1893–1979), perhaps the most widely admired of all modern Orthodox theologians. Philaret's *Catechism* reflected a shift from a scholastic way of doing theology to one more in line with the patristic writers, and has the great merit of addressing directly issues of disagreement with other Christian traditions.

After only a few lines, the *Catechism*'s first two quotations from Scripture are introduced by 'as the Word of God testifies'.[2] 'Holy Scripture' is defined as 'Certain books written by the Spirit of God through men sanctified by God, called Prophets and Apostles'.[3] Philaret accepts as canonical the same Old Testament books as evangelicals would, rejecting books such as Wisdom because they do not appear in the Hebrew Scriptures, although he follows Athanasius in acknowledging the value of reading them to those being instructed for baptism.[4] Unlike Philaret, Orthodox churches generally include the deuterocanonical books in their canon of Scripture, but often they are regarded as being on a lower level than the rest of the Old Testament.[5] Although the matter is not beyond debate, these books are an important source for Orthodox liturgical offices. It is also important to note that within Orthodoxy, translations both from the Septuagint (which includes many of the Apocryphal books) and from modern critical editions of the Hebrew and Greek texts are used.

Most of the space in the *Catechism* is devoted to enumerating Scripture's several parts and their distinctive character. Its answers ring with a confidence that would gladden an evangelical heart. The Psalms, for example, contain 'many prophecies of our Saviour Christ' and form 'a perfect manual of prayer and praise'.[6] The good tidings of the gospels tell of 'the Divinity of our Lord Jesus Christ, of his advent and life on earth, of his miracles and saving doctrine, and finally, of his death upon the cross, his glorious resurrection and ascension into heaven'.[7] Men and women could have 'no better nor more joyful tidings than these, of a Divine Saviour and everlasting salvation'.[8]

It would be an easy task to cite evangelical doctrinal statements that likewise attest the origin of Scripture in the inspiration of God. The Doctrinal Basis of the Evangelical Alliance, for instance, affirms 'the divine inspiration of the Holy Scripture and its consequent entire trustworthiness and supreme authority in all matters of faith and conduct'. That of its counterpart in the United States, the National Association of Evangelicals, asserts 'We believe the Bible to be the inspired, the only infallible, authoritative Word of God.' It is in this divine origination of Scripture that Evangelicalism has commonly rested its character as the word of God, its supreme authority and its truthfulness.

## ii) Scripture, revelation and tradition

Differences emerge between Orthodox and evangelicals when they relate Scripture to divine revelation. Evangelicals sometimes give the impression of holding that the goal of salvation-history was the production of a book. If pressed, they acknowledge that behind the Bible lies that history, in Israel and in Christ, in which divine revelation and human salvation were accomplished once and for all. Yet in their insistence that Scripture remains now the only means of access to that original salvation-history and its God-given meaning, they have often spoken of Scripture itself as divine revelation. It is the unique divinely warranted record and interpretation of the original revelation and as such partakes of the character of divine revelation itself.

Orthodoxy too speaks regularly of Scripture as accurately preserving divine revelation. Philaret asserts that Scripture was given so that 'divine revelation might be preserved more exactly and unchangeably'.[9] He continues: 'In holy Scripture we read the words of the Prophets and Apostles precisely as if we were living with them and listening to them.'

Nevertheless, Orthodoxy also characteristically distinguishes between divine revelation and Scripture. Philaret describes the latter as one of 'two channels' by which the divine revelation given historically is preserved and spread.[10] The other is 'holy tradition'. Although Philaret's distinction between 'two channels' is now not so common, we here encounter a supremely important dimension of Orthodox Christianity. We may start our examination of this by giving Philaret's next two articles.

> By the name of holy tradition is meant the doctrine of the faith, the law of
> God, the sacraments, and the ritual as handed down by the true believers and
> worshippers of God by word and example from one to another, and from
> generation to generation . . .
>   All true believers united by the holy tradition of the faith, collectively and
> successively, by the will of God, compose the Church; and she is the sure
> repository of holy tradition.[11]

Tradition is a subject that recent theological discussion, not least in
ecumenical circles, has clarified by proposing three distinct
meanings. The World Council of Churches' Montreal Faith and
Order conference in 1963, in which Orthodox representatives took
part, reported helpfully on this issue. *First*, the Tradition (with a
capital) is the gospel of God's revelation and self-giving in Christ,
transmitted down the generations in and by the Church in its
preaching of the word, its ministry of the sacraments, its witness and
service; *second*, tradition (without a capital) is the traditionary
process by which the Tradition is handed on; *third*, traditions
(without a capital and in the plural) are different confessional or
denominational traditions, such as Lutheran and Anglican (or
perhaps evangelical and liberal), or the diversity of forms of
expression in different cultures.

It is useful to set the present review of Scripture and tradition in
Orthodoxy and Evangelicalism in this context. If we pick up the
threefold distinction between the Tradition, tradition and traditions,
an acute question arises about where to place Scripture. Evangelicals
would be inclined to make it part of the Tradition itself (in the first
Montreal sense). That is to say, in terms of a distinction made by the
Swiss New Testament scholar, Oscar Cullmann, the apostles, and
hence apostolic Scripture, belong to the time of Christ rather than
the age of the church. Scripture is part of the 'once-for-all'
givenness of the momentous act of God that was Jesus Christ. This
is not to deny that the canon of Scripture, chiefly of the New
Testament, was determined within the life of the church of the first
three or four centuries – a church already developing certain
doctrinal emphases and practices which many evangelicals have
judged inconsistent with Scripture. But Cullmann's approach would
insist that the early church, in forming the Bible as we know it, did

not confer authority on its books but rather recognized their intrinsic apostolic authority. God's word written was convincing the Church of its God-given authority.

It is through this written word of God by his Spirit that God rules in his Church. This is the burden of the Protestant slogan 'Scripture alone'. This phrase does not imagine that Scripture ever exists in isolation from particular historical and cultural contexts (tradition and traditions in the second and third senses). What it means is that the word of God written is the judge of all other teachings and traditions.

But where would Orthodoxy place Holy Scripture in the threefold mapping of tradition sketched above? If we note again the teaching of the Philaret's *Catechism*, then the divine revelation is the Tradition, which is transmitted and disseminated by the two channels of 'holy tradition and holy Scripture'.[12] Yet the next two articles suggest that Orthodox faith may not fit too neatly into this threefold distinction:

> By the name holy tradition is meant the doctrine of the faith, the law of God . . . as handed down . . .
> All true believers united by the holy tradition of the faith . . . compose the Church; and she is the sure repository of holy tradition.[13]

There are subtle depths to the Orthodox understanding of Tradition and of Scripture's place in it which evangelicals are likely to find difficult to fathom. This is partly because they have been reared with an instinctive dichotomy in their minds between Scripture and tradition, shaped by controversy with Rome; we have seen that not all Orthodox operate with such a dichotomy (neither, for that matter, do many modern Catholics).

Although the Orthodox recognize the difference between traditions (e.g. between distinctive Greek and Russian ways of doing things), their instinct is to regard the traditionary process (by which certain teachings and practices are handed on) as the Tradition. It is obvious from Philaret's *Catechism* that 'the holy tradition' does more than merely transmit that which was originally given. The latter – the divine revelation – may be said to have given birth to that Tradition which stands in organic unbroken continuity with the original revelation, more specifically with Christ and his apostles. That Tradition is carried by, embodied in and in a true sense identified with the Orthodox Church. It is contained in Scripture but also in the Liturgy, the writings of the Fathers and the deliverances of the seven Ecumenical Councils. Although it has been asserted that the definitions of these councils together with Scripture 'form the absolute basis of the doctrine and practice of the whole of Orthodox Christendom',[14] these do not exhaust what Orthodoxy holds as sacrosanct.

Evangelicals wishing to grasp an understanding of Orthodox beliefs about Scripture and Tradition find that no one text or treatment sets out a definitive view. This follows, in fact, from the Orthodox conviction that Tradition can be understood as the life of the Spirit in the Church.[15] The Spirit is the ultimate source of all authority in the Church; he inspired the Scriptures and inspires the living church. Thus the Orthodox prefer to speak of a single stream of divine Tradition rather than two channels. The sources are the Holy Scriptures, the patristic, liturgical and conciliar texts, and contemporary teachers who set out faithfully to expound those sources and thereby have won authority within the Orthodox community.

It is almost impossible to conceive of Orthodoxy producing a comprehensive up-to-date compendium of Orthodox belief like the recent *Catechism of the Catholic Church*, quite apart from the fact that Orthodoxy is a family of churches. For the Orthodox, Orthodoxy is diffused and preserved not merely in texts but also in practices, in the worshipping life of a community which, not least in the Liturgy, believes itself to stand in living continuity with the apostles. As one writer has put it:

> For the Orthodox Church, the mediation of grace through the sacraments, the changing of the bread and wine into the body and blood [of Christ] as well as the sacrificial character of the Eucharist, the apostolic succession of bishops and priests, the reverencing and invocation of the Mother of God and of the saints, the efficacy of prayers for the departed, are all obligatory norms of belief, even though they have never been defined as dogma by any Council.[16]

Nor, evangelicals would want to add, are most of these beliefs consistent with Scripture, though the Orthodox would disagree, insisting that all dogmas have a biblical basis. Orthodoxy maintains that the Ecumenical Councils 'established no new doctrines not already contained in the revelation'.[17] This assertion can be meaningfully glossed, in respect of at least some of these councils' definitions, only by talking of their drawing out the implications of Scripture, implications which others would contest. But Orthodoxy has not favoured theories of the 'development' of doctrine which in Roman Catholicism have allowed latter-day dogmatic definitions such as the Immaculate Conception of Mary.

Philaret's *Catechism* teaches that holy Tradition is more ancient and original than Scripture, since Christ wrote nothing and the apostles taught orally at first.[18] Since, as we have seen, Scripture was given for the more exact and unchangeable preservation of the divine revelation,[19] the question then arises whether, once Scripture is available, it is necessary to follow holy Tradition. The answer is that 'We must follow that tradition which agrees with the divine revelation and with holy Scripture, as is taught us by holy Scripture itself' (quoting 2 Thes. 2:15).[20] Tradition is necessary even now, as 'a guide to the right understanding of holy Scripture, for the right ministration of the sacraments, and the preservation of sacred rites and ceremonies in the purity of their original institution'.[21] There follows a quotation not from the Bible but from St Basil, on liturgical and devotional practices not found in Scripture but transmitted by unwritten tradition from the apostles.[22]

The *Catechism* of Philaret does not give an integrated account of the inter-relationships this chapter has been considering. Nevertheless it is sufficiently representative of Orthodox belief for our purposes. Much more remains to be said of the role of the Tradition in the true interpretation of Scripture. On matters defined by the councils, that interpretation is not in doubt, although presumably there may be debate about what one or other council actually decided. But, as we have seen, dimensions of the Tradition beyond these councils may be said to reflect a diffused *magisterium* (formal teaching office) at work.

## iii) Scripture and the Church

Evangelicals will not accord to 'the consensus of the church' the authoritative voice it exercises in Orthodoxy. *Ecclesia reformata* ('a church reformed') speaks of a historical experience which is irreversible – of a late-medieval Catholic Church whose consensus so denied or obscured the apostolic gospel that reform at the cost of division was the sole path of obedience. The magnitude of that defining experience has tempted some evangelicals to remain in the sixteenth, or at least the seventeenth, century. But with *reformata* goes *semper reformanda* ('continually in need of, and open to, reform'). The appeal to 'Scripture alone' was forged in the face of a consensus that would not or could not reform itself. None of Evangelicalism's own traditions are exempt from the scrutiny of 'Scripture alone'. Nor, we would humbly say, are those of Orthodoxy.

Protestantism, particularly Evangelicalism, has been called 'the religion of the Book'. This could not be said in the same way of Orthodoxy. In Evangelicalism the Bible has been central in worship and the fundamental source of spiritual nourishment in private devotion. In Orthodoxy, private Bible reading is secondary to, and flows out of, encounter with the Bible in the worship of the Church: Orthodox believers are exposed in the Liturgy to a solid diet of the reading, chanting and singing of Scripture. Thus Scripture has its place firmly within the life of the community; the question, however, is whether the power of the Spirit enables Scripture to stand over against the Church and to judge it. In practice this may be an acute question for evangelical church life also, but at least evangelicals give theoretical recognition to the authority of Scripture as supreme over all other claims to truth and obedience, even if they too often fall short in putting it into practice.

Whereas Evangelicalism's argument with Protestant liberalism has pitted the voice of God in Scripture over against the supremacy of human reason as criterion of truth, with Orthodoxy, as in a different way with Catholicism, it is the relation between Scripture and church that comes into contention. The absence of a counterpart to the Reformation in Orthodox history means that the two traditions, Orthodox and evangelical, have been shaped by different sets of questions and challenges. Yet in a globally small world, after the collapse of Communism, Orthodox and evangelicals no longer live in separate houses virtually sealed off from each other. The Orthodox fear that Evangelicalism's 'the Bible alone' leads to individualism and divisiveness, and church history indicates that the fear is not wholly misplaced. Evangelicals in turn fear that the Orthodox emphasis on the normative status of churchly tradition muffles the voice of the Spirit speaking in Scripture.

### iv) Challenges for Orthodox and evangelicals

The first goal of this study is progress in understanding each other. Evangelicals are called to take more seriously the place that Scripture has in the self-understanding of Orthodoxy and in its traditions of worship and discipleship. They must also give due weight to St Paul's appeals to the 'tradition' which his converts received from him (e.g. 1 Cor. 11:2, 1 Thes. 3:6) and his insistence on the need to pass it on to those who will in turn be able to teach others (2 Tim. 2:2). The Orthodox, on the other hand, should reckon with the various checks and balances, many of them inherited from the formative eras that have classically shaped the identities of churches, that prevent evangelicals' personal access to the Scriptures from foundering on individualism. Most evangelicals read the Bible, often without recognizing it, within the safety net, as it were, of a confessional community, even if they would not formally grant that community an authority superior to that of Scripture when rightly understood.[23]

But may evangelicals and Orthodox go beyond an increase in mutual understanding and learn from each other? This learning process is likely to follow along the same tracks pursued in the interests of deeper comprehension of each other. Evangelicals have surely much more to appreciate about the Scriptures as God's gift to the Church, to be treasured and even reverenced by it in the twenty-first century as part of the extraordinarily rich heritage received from almost two millennia of Christians working on the

Bible: copyists of manuscripts, preachers and commentators, translators and printers, monks preserving and transmitting the sacred volumes, reformers vindicating the freedom of vernacular translations and public proclamation, Bible societies and many others. The Scriptures always have been God's gift *to* the Church *through* the Church. Fuller awareness of this must encourage a stronger communal dimension in evangelical study and teaching of the Scriptures.

The Orthodox, for their part, have much more to appreciate about the freedom of God's written word in directly addressing, rebuking and correcting – as well as nourishing – the Church of Christ. Ecclesiastical conservatism, liturgical captivity, cultural conformity and even linguistic traditionalism form part of the perception of the Orthodox held by many evangelicals in the United Kingdom. On these matters, evangelicals may ask whether the Orthodox are open to hear the word of the living God in Scripture. If the solitary monk is fed by patient study of the Scriptures, where is the parallel in the experience of the Orthodox congregation at worship? And what of the encouragement of personal and family Bible reading day by day, a practice which, in spite of official encouragement, is sometimes condemned at the parish level as being what the 'sects' do?

Thus evangelicals and the Orthodox may not only move to deeper respect for each other but together foster, amid the religious chaos of a post-Christian postmodernism, a more faithful reception and declaration of God's word.

## Notes

1 It is here quoted from the translation in Philip Schaff, *The Creeds of Christendom* (London: Hodder & Stoughton, 1877), vol. 2, pp. 445–542.

2 Philaret, *Catechism*, Arts. 4, 5.

3 Art. 19.

4 Arts. 33–35.

5 There is some variation between different Orthodox jurisdictions as to which books are included in the Apocrypha. A glance at the contents page

of a translation such as the *New Revised Standard Version* will show which books are accepted by which churches.

6 Art. 42.

7 Art. 47.

8 Art. 48.

9 Art. 22.

10 Art. 16.

11 Arts. 17, 18.

12 Art. 16.

13 Arts. 17, 18.

14 Wilhelm Niesel, *Reformed Symbolics* (Edinburgh: Oliver & Boyd, 1962), p. 125.

15 Vladimir Lossky, quoted by Kallistos Ware, *The Orthodox Church* (Harmondsworth: Pelican, 1997), p. 195.

16 F. Heiler, cited by Niesel, p. 126.

17 Doktussov, cited by Niesel, p. 125.

18 Philaret, *Catechism*, art. 21.

19 Art. 22.

20 Art. 23.

21 Art. 24.

22 For this quotation, see p. 20 above.

23 For a thorough comparison of evangelical and Orthodox hermeneutics, see Grant R. Osborne, 'The Many and the One: The Interface between Orthodox and Evangelical Protestant Hermeneutics', St *Vladimir's Theological Quarterly* 3 (1995), 281–304.

# 9

# Worship

Of all the comparisons to be drawn between Orthodoxy and Evangelicalism, few are more striking than those which concern worship. Evangelical theologians and commentators regularly acknowledge the centrality of worship for Christian faith and life.[1] Worship cannot, however, be said to *define* and *distinguish* Evangelicalism in the way that it defines and distinguishes Orthodoxy; moreover, worship is much less uniform in Evangelicalism than it is in Orthodoxy, and so we have not attempted to describe it in detail for Orthodox readers. This chapter therefore focuses on describing Orthodox worship, noting evangelical reactions to particular aspects along the way.

## i) Orthodoxy: a liturgical community

Many writers have attempted to describe evangelical Christianity, but none has remotely considered depicting it as an intrinsically or fundamentally 'liturgical' phenomenon.[2] This is because evangelicals do not share a particular tradition of worship. Orthodoxy is held together to a remarkable extent by the common structure of its liturgies, whereas evangelicals may be found among 'high church' Lutherans, extemporizing Pentecostals and non-sacramental Salvationists. This diversity reflects the fact that while evangelicals may value worship in *theological* terms, they regard its specific *form* and *practice* as secondary issues. Evangelicalism typically makes 'right doctrine' prior to 'right worship'. Whereas evangelicals tend to regard worship as one *reflection* of biblically based theology, in Orthodoxy it is seen more as the prism through which all theology is *refracted*.[3] When an Anglican minister asked Patriarch Alexii of Moscow to describe the Orthodox Church in a sentence, he was famously told, 'It is the church which celebrates the Divine Liturgy.'[4]

It should be made clear that when Orthodox writers refer to 'the Divine Liturgy', they specifically mean the Eucharist, rather than the full diet of worship conducted in their churches. The Liturgy used by Chalcedonian Orthodox today usually follows the Byzantine Rite, partly because of the influence of the Byzantine Empire upon local liturgical development. This rite is in fact a family of liturgies, including the ancient orders of St Basil the Great and St John Chrysostom, as well as the less frequently used orders of St James and of St Gregory of Rome (the 'Liturgy of the Pre-Sanctified Gifts').[5] The Liturgy of St John Chrysostom is the most common, being celebrated every Sunday and every holiday of the year except during Lent, when the St Gregory rite prevails on weekdays and the Liturgy of St Basil on Sundays and other special occasions, and on the Feast of St James, when the Liturgy of St James is used. The Liturgy of St Mark the Evangelist is sometimes also included as part of the Byzantine Liturgy. This is celebrated in Alexandria on St Mark's Feast Day (April 25th). Some of the local rites mentioned above are now seeing more frequent use in the jurisdictions where they appeared.[6]

Orthodox worship in the wider sense also includes the Divine Offices (such as Matins, Vespers and Compline) and Occasional Offices such as Baptism, Marriage and Burial of the Dead, all of which show a measure of ethnic and regional variation.

The names given to the various liturgies point to an important aspect of Orthodox worship: it is seen as being in the theological and liturgical succession of the worship of the early Christian centuries. While recent liturgical scholarship has often questioned the hypothesis that early Christian worship was the same in form everywhere and can be reconstructed today on the basis of surviving evidence, it is nevertheless the case that significant elements of Orthodox worship have their roots in practices of the early Christians.

Before we examine how specific elements in Orthodox liturgy diverge from evangelical approaches, we must recognize that many (though by no means all) evangelicals would be uncomfortable with the very word 'liturgy' itself, which they would apply to forms of worship such as the Anglican *Book of Common Prayer*. Often this is because of a belief that the freedom of the Spirit to inspire and enable those who lead the congregation in worship is hindered by the use of set forms of prayer. The Greek term *leitourgia*, which has the etymological connotation of 'work done by, or on behalf of, the people' and which became a technical term in the East for 'public worship', would usually be rendered 'service'; hence it is far more natural to talk of evangelical 'services' than evangelical 'liturgies'.

## ii) Evangelical worship as word-centred

Although Luther translated the Latin Mass into the vernacular, he retained its essential structure and content. By contrast, Calvin insisted that the word of God should be the sole admissible source for the form and content of worship – that 'no other word [was] to be held as the Word of God, and given place as such, in the Church'.[7] His revision of worship was born of a conviction that Rome had added numerous 'useless rites' and 'vain repetitions' to the models of worship laid down in the Bible.[8] These models were not to be seen so much as fixed forms of words or 'common prayers', but rather as core structures or 'common orders' – frameworks around which to build services suited to particular congregations. It should also be realized that once Zwingli had convened an extempore 'Service of the word' distinct from Holy Communion in Zurich at Easter 1525, a precedent was set for the Reformers to downgrade the Eucharist itself in favour of proclamation and less formally structured approaches to worship. This was reinforced by the Geneva magistrates when they reduced the frequency of the Lord's Supper from a weekly to a quarterly celebration (albeit very much against Calvin's wishes).

The legacy of this 'turn to the word' is evident today in the more verbal nature of evangelical worship as compared with that of Orthodoxy. Although Orthodox worship is admittedly full of words, it also includes features which are largely foreign to evangelical worship as traditionally practised, such as the burning of incense, veneration of icons, the signing of the cross, prostration and processions. While the sermon was until recently almost the only essential feature of an evangelical church service, it is but one element among many in Orthodox worship, and hardly as central as the Eucharist. Indeed, no formal provision is made for it in the Liturgy. If there is a sermon, it is often delivered in the form of a short homily, rather than in the more oratorical, expository style prevalent in Evangelicalism (though there was an Antiochene tradition of expository preaching, exemplified by St John Chrysostom, who preached through various books of the Bible verse by verse).[9]

### iii) Orthodox worship as a 'representation' of salvation history

One reason for this difference of emphasis is that the core purpose of Orthodox liturgy is to 're-present' Christ (dramatizing and re-enacting the history of salvation) through the worship of the congregation and the performance of the Eucharist, whereas evangelicals view the church service much more as a means to expounding and 'memorializing' truths *already* and *once for all* mediated through Jesus' life, death and resurrection, and through the completed canon of Scripture. So in evangelical services it is normal to have little or no division between minister and congregation, communion table and nave, because believers have *already* been reconciled to God through the death and resurrection of Christ, whereas for the Orthodox it is salutary to *re-experience* how that reconciliation came about, through the actions of the Eucharist. In Orthodox thinking, the Divine Liturgy realizes a communion of heaven and earth which was broken through sin but restored by Christ.

As well as re-presenting salvation-history, Orthodox worship is seen as a real participation in the ongoing worship of heaven. Those who participate in the Liturgy enter a celebration which is not only local, or even global, but heavenly and cosmic; as the words spoken at the Great Entrance in the Liturgy of the Presanctified express it, 'Now the celestial powers are present with us, and worship invisibly.' This 'presencing' of heaven is supremely realized by the 'real presence' of Christ in the bread and wine of the Eucharist.[10]

## iv) Orthodox Liturgy in its setting

In so far as Orthodoxy places great emphasis on the gathered congregation, it bears certain similarities with most evangelical traditions (including charismatic ones). The fact that its principal services are organized as single events for the whole community, rather than being divided into various smaller gatherings throughout the day, reflects the approach taken by the majority of evangelical churches. Indeed, the Orthodox hold it as a common principle that no Holy Table[11] which has been used to celebrate the Eucharist can be employed again for the same purpose on the same day.

There are, however, significant contrasts. For one thing, seating is traditionally absent from Orthodox church buildings and the congregation stands throughout,[12] although some provision may be made for the elderly and infirm, with benches placed around the edges of the nave. As Ware describes it, the lack of chairs or pews lends Orthodox worship 'a flexibility' and 'unselfconscious informality' which is rare among traditional Western congregations:

'Western worshippers, ranged in their neat rows, all in their proper places, cannot move about the service without causing a disturbance; a western congregation is generally expected to arrive at the beginning and to stay to the end. But in Orthodox worship people can come and go far more freely, and nobody is greatly surprised if they move about during the service.'[13] Indeed, at many points, especially in the earlier part of the Liturgy, worshippers may be found kissing icons, lighting candles, offering rolls of bread and handing lists of names for prayer to the deacon.[14]

## a) The divide between clergy and laity

While such activity might appear distracting to many evangelicals, it is a consequence of Orthodoxy's much sharper division between the functions and roles of clergy and people in worship. So great is the distinction, in fact, that the appearance of Orthodox worship has even been described as that of 'two services conducted simultaneously' – one performed by the priests and largely inaudible to the people, and the other by the congregation.[15] Not only do Orthodox priests identify themselves by wearing distinctive vestments, whereas many evangelical clergy tend to reject liturgical dress altogether or restrict it to a minimum, they also spend up to an hour preparing the Eucharistic elements in a side chapel before appearing in the main part of the church. This reinforces the special status of the priest in relation to the Liturgy: he is understood to be a mediator of Christ's presence, along with the bread and wine themselves. This comes as a shock to those evangelicals who are used to lay leadership of services, and even lay presidency at communion. However, it should be balanced with the recognition that the priest is viewed as celebrating the Liturgy with, and as part of, the people; Orthodoxy does not have the private celebrations found in Roman Catholicism.

Even when the public rite begins, evangelicals would be surprised at the division of clergy and laypeople. Every Orthodox Liturgy is chanted, and it is the priests and deacons who often take responsibility for the chanting, which is unaccompanied by musical instruments. Lay choirs or chanters are also used (as are lay readers and male lay assistants in the Altar), and more recent moves have been made in some quarters towards congregational participation in the chanting. However, such a trend is not universal, and is in any case far removed from the congregational singing of hymns and songs which has done so much to define the shape and character of evangelical worship, and the more recent encouragement of the practice of 'open prayer', a period in the service during which any member of the congregation may pray audibly.

Beyond all this, the most obvious divide between clergy and people is represented by the *iconostasis*, the screen on which the icons are displayed, and which separates the sanctuary, accessed by the priests in various parts of the Liturgy, from the main body of the church, where the faithful gather. In Orthodox understanding, the *iconostasis* bears deep theological significance. While evangelicals would characteristically see it as threatening their commitment to the priesthood of all believers and the demystification of ritual, some Orthodox regard it as signifying a very genuine division. Thus, for one modern writer,

> 'The Holy Doors show that God has come to bring us back to Him. We are reunited with God by Christ and His teaching. When it is time for Communion, the Holy Doors are opened wide and the priest comes through the doorway with the chalice. The earth and heaven are joined once again.'[16]

This explanation typifies the sense in which the Orthodox conceive the Liturgy as dramatizing and re-enacting the history of salvation, and compares markedly with the evangelical tendency to view worship as a 'memorialization' of events which have already taken place. The closest parallel in evangelical worship is the elevation of the pulpit from which the preacher declares authoritatively the living word of God. By the power of the Holy Spirit at work through the word, God deals directly with human beings and meets the spiritual needs of those who believe.

## b) Icons

As its name suggests, the *iconostasis* is covered with icons, 'holy pictures' of Christ and the saints designed to provide a focus and stimulus to worship. A key role in Orthodox worship and devotion is played by icons. They became an important part of personal devotion by the sixth or seventh century, but lengthy and bitter controversy about them led to the calling of a council at Nicea in 787. This dealt with two distinct issues: (a) the legitimacy of depicting Christ at all, and (b) the legitimacy of offering physical veneration to icons. One side, the Iconoclasts, denied both, while the other, the Iconodules, accepted both. Although the controversy was not concluded until 843, the Iconodules were ultimately victorious. Their victory is celebrated on the First Sunday of Lent, which marks the 'Triumph of Orthodoxy'.

Icons appear all over Orthodox churches – on walls, in shrines, on desks and on tables throughout the nave. The most important, however, are those on the *iconostasis*. On either side of the Holy Door in the middle of it are icons of Christ and of Mary holding the infant Christ in her arms. On the gates there is the icon of the Annunciation, and beneath this icons of the four Evangelists. Many evangelicals fear that the adornment of churches with icons and their use in worship could lead to idolatry, but the Orthodox justify them in terms of the incarnation, and the 'divinization' of the world which resulted from it. St John of Damascus (c. 675–749), in his classic defence of icons, explains this:

> In former times God, who is without form or body, could never be depicted. But now when God is seen in the flesh conversing with men, I make an image of the God whom I see. I do not worship matter; I worship the Creator of matter who became matter for my sake, who willed to take his abode in matter; who worked out my salvation through matter. Never will I cease honouring the matter which wrought my salvation![17]

In this conception, an icon represents nothing less than a 'sacrament', a 'window into heaven' which makes visible the presence of the whole company of heaven and unites heavenly and earthly 'Liturgy'.[18]

St John of Damascus pointed out that just as the material elements of the Eucharist, and other material objects such as crosses and relics, could be the vehicles for spiritual grace, so too could icons. Just as it was appropriate to venerate these other material objects, so too icons might also be venerated, the honour passing to the one whom these things symbolized:

> Is not the life-giving altar made of matter? From it we receive the bread of life! Are not gold and silver matter? From them we make crosses, patens, chalices! And over and above all these things, is not the Body and Blood of our Lord matter? Either do away with the honour and veneration these things deserve, or accept the tradition of the Church and the veneration of images.[19]

This sacramental view of icons is played out in the physical devotion paid to them. Worshippers will kiss them; they may also hold infants up to them to wait for a blessing from the saint depicted. Icons are illuminated by candles lit in front of them. Worshippers may cross themselves before an icon, or bow in veneration to it. Icons are used not only in churches, but also in homes, and as such they provide an important connection between congregational and domestic worship – a connection which is often as strong as that maintained in Evangelicalism by very different means (see Ch. 10).

Orthodox veneration of icons presents a major stumbling block for evangelicals. Indeed, Os Guinness speaks for many when he describes evangelicals as 'unashamedly iconoclasts' – that is, wedded to a word-based understanding of the faith rather than to an image-based view of Christianity. Commenting on the increasingly visual 'captivity' of the televised and computerized West, he warns evangelicals not to be seduced by 'the corruption of Eastern Orthodoxy in the fifth century and Roman Catholicism in the fourteenth century, [which] maintained that a shift from the Word to the image would be an effective way of bringing the Word and Sacrament to everyone', but which led to a 'repression of the Word' and to an excess of 'mystical theology'.[20]

Although this viewpoint is probably still representative of the evangelical mainstream, younger and more radical evangelicals have begun to adopt a more open – if qualified – attitude towards the use of visual elements in worship. This has been especially noticeable in the so-called 'alternative worship' wing of Evangelicalism, in which the use of icons has become increasingly popular.[21] Lutherans have always accepted the legitimacy of depicting Christ and the saints in iconic form, if not the veneration of icons, and some Reformed thinkers are coming to similar conclusions.[22]

## c) Relics

Orthodox worship is further made concrete through the use of relics. These are objects which serve as memorials of the lives of the saints – either parts of their bodies or special items such as their clothing. Just as icons are perceived to bear something of the grace which characterized the lives of the saints they depict, so relics are taken to mediate holiness in a similar way, and are venerated accordingly. As with icons, they are sometimes linked to miraculous healings and revelations. Although biblical warrant is sought for them in the story of Elijah's bones (2 Kgs. 13:21), and in the cloths touched by Paul (Acts 19:12), relics have long been dismissed by evangelicals as tools of superstition. Wyclif and Hus called them idolatrous, and Calvin rejected their use as a 'heathenish custom'.[23]

### d) Incense

Another aspect of Orthodox worship which makes it more sensory than evangelical worship is the use of incense. Sometimes justified from Malachi 1:11 and Psalm 141:2, this practice has characterized the Byzantine Rite for most of its history. Censing (the swinging of a bowl on a chain containing burning incense) takes place at various points throughout the Divine Liturgy, being directed not only towards the Eucharistic elements and icons, but also towards the worshippers themselves, on the basis that they are created in God's image and are thus bearers of divinity. Evangelical polemic against incense has not generally been as strong as against icons or relics, but it would typically be regarded as another unwarranted distraction from the word.

### e) Other aspects

Veneration of the physical includes the elements used in the Eucharist. When the offerings are brought to the Altar in procession and placed on the Holy Table, they are sometimes venerated by the congregation in ways which would again draw charges of idolatry from many evangelicals (e.g. bowing and prostration).

Beyond the Divine Liturgy, certain other features of Orthodox worship deserve mention. While many evangelicals belong to churches which baptize infants, the Orthodox practice of immersing infants three times and then giving them communion is distinctive. Whereas Orthodox say prayers for the dead in a special corner of the church containing a bowl of grain to symbolize the 'imperishable seed' of a redeemed life, such prayers were rejected by the Reformers as undermining the doctrine of justification by faith, and they do not form part of evangelical worship. All the same, the Orthodox do not usually relate this practice to the decidedly un-evangelical doctrine of purgatory, unlike those whom the Reformers opposed. Furthermore, Orthodox priests hear confessions, whereas confession is understood by most evangelicals as something made directly to God in prayer.

In addition to architectural features already noted, there are aspects of Orthodox church design which ensure greater regularity of layout than in evangelical buildings. The nave is square rather than rectangular, and is usually topped by a dome rather than a spire, steeple or tower. This dome is decorated internally with images of Christ, the prophets, apostles and angels, and scenes from the New Testament. The sanctuary behind the *iconostasis* is arranged as a semi-circular apse. The Holy Table is mostly square in shape and topped with a cross and candlesticks. All this adds to the 'dramatization' of the gospel in the liturgy, and contributes to the Orthodox view that their church buildings are *themselves* profoundly sacramental, making heaven a reality on earth. As such, it reinforces what has become very clear in this brief survey: that despite certain similarities with Evangelicalism, and some aspects shared over against Rome, Orthodox worship is considerably more symbolic, ritualistic, priestly and uniform than that of evangelical churches.

## Notes

1 E.g. James Montgomery Boice, *Foundations of the Christian Faith: A Comprehensible and Readable Theology* (Leicester: IVP, 1986), pp. 587–93; Edmund P. Clowney, 'The Biblical Theology of the Church', in D. A. Carson (ed.), *The Church in the Bible and the World* (Grand Rapids, MI: Baker / Carlisle: Paternoster, 1987), pp. 16–27; Wayne Grudem, *Systematic Theology: An Introduction to Christian Doctrine* (Leicester: IVP, 1994), pp. 1003–15; John R. W. Stott, *Christ the Controversialist: A Study in Some Essentials of Evangelical Religion* (London: Tyndale Press, 1970), p. 160.

2 Cf. D. W. Bebbington, *Evangelicalism in Modern Britain: A history from the 1970s to the 1980s* (London: Unwin Hyman, 1989), pp. 1–19; Alister McGrath, *Evangelicalism and the Future of Christianity* (London: Hodder & Stoughton, 1993), pp. 49–88; Timothy R. Phillips and Dennis L. Okholm, *Welcome to the Family: An Introduction to Evangelical Christianity* (Wheaton, IL: Bridgepoint, 1996), pp. 13–15; Derek J. Tidball, *Who are the Evangelicals? Tracing the Roots of the Modern Movements* (Basingstoke: Marshall Pickering, 1994), pp. 7–18.

3 For elaboration of this point see George Every, *The Byzantine Patriarchate* (London: SPCK, 1947).

4 Cited by Sergei Hackel, 'Orthodox Worship', in J. G. Davies (ed.), *A New Dictionary of Liturgy and Worship* (London: SCM, 1986), p. 421.

5 For English-language editions of the Divine Liturgy see *The Divine Liturgy of Our Father among the Saints John Chrysostom* (Oxford: Oxford University Press, 1995), for a modern-language translation, with parallel English and Greek text; *The Orthodox Liturgy* (Oxford: Oxford University Press, 1982); Fellowship of St Alban and St Sergius, *The Orthodox Liturgy* (London: SPCK, 1939).

For studies of the Liturgy see Nicolas Cabasilas (tr. J. M. Hussy & P. A. McNulty), *Commentary on the Divine Liturgy* (London: SPCK, 1960), an important fourteenth-century Greek work; Alexander Schmemann, *An Introduction to Liturgical Theology* (London: Faith Press, 1966); and *For the Life of the World* (Crestwood, NY: St Vladimir's Seminary, 1988); Hans-Joachim Schulz (tr. Matthew O'Connell), *The Byzantine Liturgy, Symbolic Structure and Faith Expression* (New York: Pueblo, 1986); Hugh Wybrew, *The Orthodox Liturgy: The Development of the Eucharistic Liturgy in the Byzantine Rite* (London: SPCK, 1989).

6 There are also some 'Western rite' parishes (more in North America than in the United Kingdom), which are in full communion with the Orthodox Church but which use rites based upon those which appeared in Western Christianity before the schism of 1054 (see Kallistos Ware, *The Orthodox Church* (Harmondsworth: Pelican, 1997), pp. 185–6).

7 John Calvin, *Institutes of the Christian Religion*, 4.8.8; ed. J. T. McNeill, tr. F. L. Battles (Philadelphia, PA: Westminster/London: SCM, 1960), vol. II, p. 1155.

8 Ibid. 3.20.29 (vol. II, p. 891); 4.10.19 (vol. II, p. 1198).

9 It is one of the ironies of history that Zwingli, when criticized for re-

introducing such a practice, appealed to none other than Chrysostom as a precedent.

10 While the Orthodox have argued about the propriety of the term 'transubstantiation' to describe the change which comes upon the elements, and while they are generally reluctant to define the mechanics of this change in detail, there would be widespread assent to the more general approach of Article 340 of Philaret's *Catechism*, which states that 'the bread truly, really and substantially becomes the very true Body of the Lord, and the wine the very Blood of the Lord' but without defining how this takes place. For more on the debates about 'transubstantiation' see Ware, *Church*, pp. 283–5.

11 The term 'Altar' is sometimes used by Orthodox writers to describe what most evangelicals would call the 'communion table', but 'holy table' is the more usual expression. 'Altar' usually denotes the whole area behind the *iconostasis*.

12 Ware (*Church*, p. 269) notes that this is now changing, not only in the West but even in Greece.

13 Ibid., pp. 269–70.

14 Of course, the advent of charismatic worship in Evangelicalism has modified the contrast considerably: worshippers in charismatic churches remain standing for much of the service, and while most of the congregation engage in praise some may be involved in praying with individuals with spiritual needs.

15 Wybrew, p. 9. However, it must be remembered that some of the prayers offered by the priest are his personal prayers, which may perhaps be compared with the evangelical minister praying silently in the pulpit before the sermon. The main body of the Liturgy is intended to be audible to the people.

16 Tony Holden, *Explaining Icons* (Welshpool, Powys: Stylite, 1985), p. 10.

17 John of Damascus (tr. David Anderson), *On the Divine Images* (Crestwood, NY: St Vladimir's Seminary, 1980), p. 23 ('First Apology Against Those Who Attack Divine Images', §16).

18 Ware, *Church*, pp. 271–2.

19 John of Damascus, pp. 23–4.

20 Os Guinness, 'The Word in the Age of the Image: The Challenge to Evangelicals', in Melvyn Tinker (ed.), *The Anglican Evangelical Crisis: A*

*Radical Agenda for a Bible Based Church* (Fearn: Christian Focus, 1995), pp. 167–8.

21  For an exploration of this see David Hilborn, *Picking Up the Pieces: Can Evangelicals Adapt to Contemporary Culture?* (London: Hodder & Stoughton, 1997).

22  For an example of this, see Jeffrey Myers, *Vere Homo: The Case for Pictures of Our Lord Jesus Christ* (Niceville, FL: Biblical Horizons, 1993).

23  For more background see P. D. Steeves, 'Relics', in Walter A. Elwell (ed.), *Dictionary of Evangelical Theology* (Grand Rapids, MI: Baker/Carlisle: Paternoster, 1984), p. 930.

# 10

# Prayer and Spirituality

Interest in spirituality (our relationship with God and the means by which this is developed) is at the heart of the complex of issues involved in the conversion of individuals from one group to the other. This chapter outlines the main features of evangelical and Orthodox spirituality, but coverage of evangelical spirituality focuses on its Western manifestations. Evangelical spirituality in Eastern Europe would be closer in certain aspects to that of Orthodoxy as its parent culture, notably in the greater emphasis given to the corporate dimension.[1]

## i) Evangelical spirituality: 'knowing Christ as your Saviour'

As already noted, Evangelicalism is perhaps 'as much a devotional ethos as it is a theological system'.[2] It is the 'mood' or attitude of heart in which the historic creeds are confessed. Thus it is in spirituality as much as doctrine that Evangelicalism's distinctive character is most clearly evident.

### a) Foundations of evangelical spirituality

Until recently, evangelicals did not use the term 'spirituality' very much. However, this did not mean that they were unconcerned about developing their relationship with God or attempting to give it some kind of conceptual expression. Evangelical spirituality has always sought to apply to personal experience an extensively developed soteriology, covering humanity's capacity for knowing God, human need as arising from the break in relationship with God caused by sin, and the work of Christ, with a focus on the cross rather than the incarnation or the resurrection. The doctrinal focus of evangelical spirituality is thus on redemption; often this has been at the expense of creation.

Evangelicals have what might be described as a 'twice-born' spirituality, founded on the doctrine of the new birth and the experience of conversion. Such a spirituality has three aspects, corresponding to the past, present and future uses of the verb 'save' in the New Testament and placing most emphasis on the first.

### A. The past tense: knowledge of justification

Evangelical teaching regarding human need insists that sinful human beings cannot secure salvation by merit, but must have something certain on which to rely: Christ's work and God's declaration that those who trust in this are accepted as righteous. The promises made in Scripture, the awareness of the Spirit's presence in me, and the evidence of a changed life all provide grounds for a sense of assurance that I am accepted by God as righteous in Christ, that Christ's death avails *for me* (cf. Gal. 2:20), but the most weight is given to the promises; it is the Spirit's work to create a believing response to them in our hearts.

### B. The present tense: the process of sanctification

As a host of evangelicals have insisted, God does not justify us without also beginning to sanctify us: 'faith alone saves, but the faith which saves is never alone'.[3] Good works are thus seen as evidence of saving faith (this is how many evangelicals interpret Jas. 2:14–26). There is a distinction between justification and sanctification (which evangelicals wish to safeguard), but not a division. Justification is an event standing at the beginning of the new life, and sanctification is a process which begins with justification and ends with our complete transformation into the likeness of Christ.

This process is seen as involving conflict and struggle, but also as being possible because of the Spirit's work in us.

### C. The future tense: the hope of glorification

Evangelicals assured of their acceptance by God look forward confidently to being glorified with Christ in heaven and to reflecting his likeness perfectly. This is the goal of the process of transformation into the likeness of Christ (1 Jn. 3:2–3).

## b) Evangelical spirituality in practice

Evangelical spirituality is not primarily a set of devotional practices or techniques, but the outworking of a particular understanding of Christianity. 'As Christianity is, in essence, a personal relationship between the individual and God, growth occurs naturally and uniquely in so far as the person remains open to the work of the Spirit of God within his or her life.'[4] That said, it remains true that until recently evangelical practice has remained remarkably homogeneous.

Evangelical spirituality values the active rather than the contemplative life; activism, we have noted, has been a hallmark of Evangelicalism. In particular, evangelicals have been active in seeking to win others to Christ. This activism has its down side: a recurrent tendency of evangelical spirituality has been legalism (reducing spirituality to performance of the right external actions) or a conscious reaction against it. However, in recent years there has been increased interest in such practices as retreats and meditation (usually on Scripture, and distinguished from non-Christian forms of meditation).

In many ways, evangelical spirituality is individual before it is corporate. The 'Quiet Time', a regular period of devotional Bible reading and prayer, is the primary means by which evangelicals have cultivated their relationship with God. Evangelicals are confident that the Spirit enables them to understand the Scriptures, the expectation being that Scripture will speak to *me*. They have been marked by their familiarity with the text of Scripture. Bible-reading notes or other explanatory material may be used, and what is read is turned into prayer. Personal spirituality, nourished in this way, prepares an individual to take a meaningful part in corporate worship.

Assurance that believers have a great high priest (Heb. 4:14–16) leads to boldness in prayer, notably in approaching God as Father and in petitionary prayer. This concept of God and the emphasis on 'praying to God' rather than 'saying one's prayers' help to account for evangelical preference for extempore over liturgical prayer in private devotion. Prayer is nevertheless carefully structured, through division into its various aspects, and through the use of prayer lists.

The personal nature of evangelical spirituality has resulted in a diminution of the role of the Church in fostering and resourcing spirituality. Sometimes the local church has been seen primarily as a place where non-Christians can hear the gospel. The sacraments are not generally significant in English evangelical church life today, although evangelicals in other countries (notably Scotland) and other generations have placed far more emphasis on them. More important are fellowship, corporate prayer and Bible study. Traditionally, an evangelical minister must be a preacher, preaching assuming a sacramental dimension as a *locus* for encounter with God – though this too is changing as evangelicals place increasing emphasis on other aspects of worship as part of their services, and as evangelical ministerial training becomes increasingly specialized, tailored towards producing church-planters, youth workers, worship leaders, pastoral co-ordinators and so on.

The midweek prayer meeting has usually been regarded as the source of the local church's power and the most accurate indicator of its spiritual state of health. Its main focus is on Bible study and prayer. Prayer will focus on petition and thanksgiving for answers received, with individuals offering extempore prayers. Such prayer strengthens the sense of fellowship and mutual support, but concentration on these aspects of prayer can crowd out the aspects of adoration and confession of sin. Meetings of this nature are considerably less well attended than formerly, and many evangelical churches have a programme of small group meetings in homes during the week which fulfil similar functions.

Curiously, in view of what has been said about the lack of

importance attached to the Church as a catalyst for evangelical spirituality, large gatherings have played a highly significant role in shaping the spirituality of many evangelicals. This has long been so (the 'Keswick Convention' being a classic example), but recent years have seen an explosion of the number of such events, providing for evangelicals of all varieties. They provide teaching – sometimes on specialized issues which local churches are ill-equipped to tackle or at a level which is not appropriate in the local context – fellowship, celebratory worship, a challenge to missionary involvement and also entertainment.

Sources of spiritual nourishment include *Scripture* (especially St John's Gospel and Paul's letters); *hymns and songs* (which have assumed a major catechetical role); *sermons, books and periodicals* (Evangelicalism has often been active in circulating Christian literature); and *personal example* (role models may provide spiritual direction, the prime example in traditional Evangelicalism being the pastor, who counsels, preaches and leads by example). Furthermore, evangelical spirituality is shaped as well as reflected by more ephemeral items such as greetings cards or music tapes.

### c) Varieties of evangelical spirituality

Rather than speaking of 'evangelical spirituality', it may be more accurate to think of a group of spiritualities sharing the above features. Two obvious polarities within this group would be:

- *Charismatic/non-charismatic.* The Charismatic movement and the cultural shift of which it forms a part have resulted in a greater emphasis on personal experience of the Spirit's working; increasing openness to the spiritualities of other Christian traditions; a frequent lessening of acquaintance with the Scriptures and of concern for doctrine; and a more positive estimation of the material realm as a vehicle of divine grace. Two-thirds of the membership of the Evangelical Alliance is charismatic in some sense, although a significant proportion of non-charismatic (and often non-ecumenically-aligned) evangelicals do not belong to it.
- *Calvinist/Arminian.* Although this is not always as significant in

terms of spirituality as it is doctrinally, Calvinists would place greater emphasis on a sound grasp of fundamental doctrine as an essential part of spirituality, whereas classical Arminians (such as those in the Wesleyan tradition), like their Pietist forebears, would tend to stress more the idea of 'faith working through love' (Gal. 5:6). We noted earlier that the Pietist stress on Christian experience has led to a downplaying of the importance of doctrine in certain quarters, not least as a means of overcoming the sharp doctrinal divisions within Protestantism. Calvinists derive sustenance from the doctrine of divine providence, in which God is portrayed as in sovereign control of all that happens in history and in the life of each believer, so that Calvinist spirituality is marked by the attitude of trustful submission to the will of God; Arminians fear that this doctrine engenders an unchristian fatalism which militates against effort in the quest for holiness. Of course, these emphases should not be seen as mutually exclusive, and in practice they are usually mingled to a greater or lesser extent.

In recent years Evangelicalism has appeared unsure of itself in the area of spirituality. Feeling a lack of deep-rooted spirituality in their own tradition and unaware of much of their heritage, evangelicals have plundered the resources of other Christian traditions, perhaps without stopping to reflect on the doctrinal principles which those spiritualities express.

## ii) Orthodox spirituality: 'communion with God'

### a) Foundations of Orthodox spirituality

Salvation is most naturally conceived of by the Orthodox as a *process* ('I am being saved'), rather than the evangelical *event* ('I have been saved'): 'Conversion begins but it never ends. It is an increasing process in which we gradually become more and more what we should be.'[5] Synergism is important in this: 'without God's grace we can do nothing; but without our voluntary co-operation God *will* do nothing.'[6] The supreme example of synergism is Mary: God waited for her willing response (Lk. 1:38) before becoming incarnate.[7]

Because of the emphasis on process (salvation is the *way* the disciple treads rather than the *door* of entry into discipleship), the Orthodox do not have a specific doctrine of assurance, and indeed find evangelical claims to assurance lacking in humility. Rather, their assurance is founded upon the merciful nature of God. However, St Symeon the New Theologian appears to have taught a robust understanding of Christian assurance, in some respects similar to that of Evangelicalism.

Orthodox spirituality is *apophatic*, emphasizing human inability to comprehend or define God. God is utterly transcendent; even communion with God is in some way an experience of his otherness. Yet this is balanced by an awareness of God's immanence: 'God is both further from us, and nearer to us, than anything else.'[8]

The goal is *theosis* or 'deification': the Fathers from Irenaeus onwards have taught that Christ became man that we might become divine. This participation in the divine nature (2 Pet. 1:4) or communion with God (cf. Jn. 14 – 17) is not to be understood in pantheistic terms, however, for a distinction is made between God's essence and his energies: 'The essence signifies the whole God as he is in himself; the energies signify the whole God as he is in action.'[9] Human beings participate in the latter but not the former: only Christ is Son of God by nature; we become children of God by grace. As Christ shared in our humanity, so we may share in his divinity (as qualified above) through communion with him and transformation by the Holy Spirit.[10]

### b) Orthodox spirituality in practice

Orthodox spirituality is fundamentally ecclesial. Life in the Church is to be a foretaste of salvation, and a catalyst to personal spiritual experience: 'nothing increases the fervour of inner prayer so much as being in church.'[11] The Church is the sphere in which the Spirit is especially at work. Within it the 'mysteries' (the main Orthodox term for sacraments) are administered. Through baptism the Spirit makes us members of Christ's body and confers divine life, while the Eucharist nourishes that life as 'the medicine of immortality'; thus personal spirituality is tied in with the life of the Church.

The Church is where heaven touches earth, and the Liturgy a participation in the ongoing heavenly worship: 'Truly, the temple is heaven upon earth; for where the throne of God is, where the terrible mysteries are celebrated, where the angels serve together with men, where the Almighty is unceasingly glorified, there is truly heaven, and the heaven of heavens.'[12] Thus the Orthodox have a strong belief in the communion of saints. As well as the use of icons, saints' days are celebrated, their relics venerated and their prayers besought: private prayer will end with the words 'Through the prayers of the holy fathers, Lord Jesus Christ our God, have mercy on us. Amen.'[13] The saints are those who have advanced furthest along to road to deification, and whose prayer is thus seen as especially effective. Above all is Mary, whose prayers are besought whenever an Orthodox prays.

The home is a microcosm of the Church, and an Orthodox home will have its icon corner for prayer. Daily private prayer, like corporate prayer, is primarily liturgical, though extempore prayer is also encouraged. As we have noted, to many evangelical observers Bible reading appears less important in Orthodox private devotion than in much contemporary Evangelicalism, though it is considerably more significant in corporate worship.[14] The liturgical readings are drawn largely from the Psalms in the Old Testament, and preponderantly from the four Gospels within the New Testament; the Revelation of John is never read. Yet the lives of the saints, a significant resource in Orthodox piety, often emphasize their ceaseless meditation on parts of Scripture and sometimes extensive memorization. Furthermore, the Fathers of the early church include tireless and gifted expositors of the Bible like St John Chrysostom.

Bodily discipline is seen as important in prayer in a way which is not always true of traditional Evangelicalism. As well as the use of various bodily postures, the rhythm of fasts and feasts, following the liturgical calendar, is most important to Orthodox spirituality and family life. Yet it is balanced by flexibility in application; it is the heart which matters above all else in prayer. Rhythms of place and time are balanced with the idea of prayer as constant, a prime example being the continual repetition of the Jesus Prayer, 'Lord Jesus Christ, Son of God, have mercy on me [a sinner].' This is seen as a way of bringing the imagination under control in the quest to attain a constant state of prayerfulness, free from mental images and concepts of human origin. The Jesus Prayer may be constantly repeated but Orthodox insist that it is not a mantra, because of its clear meaning: contained within it is the saving name upon which we call. 'The Jesus Prayer is not some talisman. Its power comes from faith in the Lord, and from a deep union of the mind and heart with him.'[15]

A key word describing Orthodox spirituality would be 'humility', arising from contrition: 'Progress in the spiritual life is shown by an ever-increasing realization of our own worthlessness . . . There are many good feelings, but the feeling of worthlessness is the most fundamental; and when it is absent everything else is of no use.'[16]

The idea of spiritual conflict is also important to the spirituality of a communion which sees itself as having been divinely called to suffer for the faith. Orthodox spiritual teaching displays a keen awareness of the devil's devices and the need for believers to resist him. It also stresses that they have to do battle with those aspects of themselves which are not yet in conformity with the will of God, bringing the passions under control. This must not be confused with the issue of spiritual darkness (a loss of the sense of God's presence), which the Orthodox, like evangelicals, would usually see as something to be overcome rather than a necessary stage in the way to union with God.

The chief work of monastics is that of prayer; monastic spirituality majors on the motifs of repentance and return to God. The primary requirement for monastics is thus that of holiness, and they are seen as sources of prayer and counsel for Christians in the world. Yet in many respects monastic spirituality is fundamentally *similar* to that of ordinary Christians: even the *Philokalia*, a collection of spiritual writings made on Mount Athos late in the eighteenth century and comprising works written between the fourth and fifteenth centuries, was intended to make monastic spirituality accessible for all. It achieved tremendous popularity when translated into Russian, and has become influential in the West.

### c) Sources for Orthodox spirituality

The Orthodox emphasize that the theology of the Tradition, including the Fathers and the early councils, speaks to and about Christian life; theology is no abstract academic pursuit. Two particular sources are Scripture and the Liturgy.

As noted above, Scripture forms a major part of the Liturgy, especially the Gospels and Psalms (interpreted messianically). The Orthodox are sensitive to the New Testament's ecclesiological dimension, discerning ecclesial and liturgical patterns which evangelicals often miss. Scripture is interpreted according to Tradition (see Ch. 8): 'Scripture must be understood with the mind of the Church, the mind of Christ, because the Church has not changed; in its inner experience it continues to live the same life as it lived in the first century'.[17]

Most prayers in devotional manuals are taken from the service books, demonstrating the liturgical nature of Orthodox spirituality. The individual prays as part of the Church, using its prayers and Psalms, which mould his or her spirituality as evangelicals are moulded by the hymns or songs which they sing. In both cases, the individual grows into the experiences therein expressed.

## iii) Comparative evaluation

Although some evangelicals fear that Orthodox spirituality represents 'another gospel' (Gal. 1:6–9) and some Orthodox perceive Evangelicalism as heretical novelty, lacking necessary safeguards against falling into deception, there are striking similarities between them.

## a) Similarities

Both emphasize the tie-up between theology and experience (as do many traditions): spirituality is an expression of one's doctrinal standpoint. Speaking from an Orthodox standpoint, Lossky calls mystical theology 'a spirituality which expresses a doctrinal attitude',[18] while Gordon, as an evangelical, defines spirituality as 'doctrine prayed, experienced and lived in a life of committed obedience to Christ'.[19] Thus both warn against the importation of aspects of alien spiritualities on the ground that these are founded on alien doctrinal perspectives.

Orthodoxy thinks primarily in terms of life *in* Christ, a new quality of life which the baptized experience as they are transformed into the likeness of Christ, rather than imitation of Christ. Here many evangelicals may find common ground with it (though not those whose spirituality is heavily influenced by Anabaptism).

Concerning the place of human effort in spirituality, the difference may be less than might be thought, since both traditions emphasize the need to work at growing in grace, using what God has given for the purpose.

While evangelicals sometimes accuse the Orthodox of externalism, losing sight of the stress on the importance of inner prayer, their own emphasis on activism may also result in a loss of attention to the inner sources of spiritual vitality.

## b) Differences

By contrast with evangelicals, who see Scripture as the yardstick against which the Church's doctrine and practice must always be measured, the Orthodox prefer to see Scripture and the Church as part of the Tradition which witnesses to human experience of the Spirit. Parallel to this runs their unhappiness with 'external' categories to describe our relationship with God, such as justification understood as a divine declaration which takes place outside us and apart from any human worthiness, and their preference for categories which reflect our experience of inner transformation, such as deification.

Evangelicals have alleged that the Orthodox have a less radical view of the effects of the Fall on human nature and freedom; as evidence of this they would point to the importance attached to the concept of synergy by Orthodox. In terms of historic evangelical doctrine that is certainly so, but Orthodox spiritual teaching is more searching than much modern Evangelicalism in its analysis of the deceitfulness of sin and the difficulty of overcoming it. This is a factor which has attracted some converts from Evangelicalism.

A fundamental difference between evangelical and Orthodox spirituality is pointed up by the Orthodox practice of invoking the saints. Evangelicals see no need, as those who have been accepted by God through Christ, to invoke the saints, on the ground that Christ invites them in Scripture to approach him directly (the letter to the Hebrews is particularly pertinent here). The Orthodox find it difficult to see the force of such an objection, pointing out that when evangelicals ask their fellow-believers to pray for them they do not see this as a substitute for their own access to God. However, the distinction made by many Orthodox between praying to saints and requesting the prayers of the saints is one which evangelicals often find it hard to grasp.

The Orthodox sometimes criticize popular Evangelicalism as having a 'minimalist' approach to salvation, concerned only with the minimum necessary to avoid the prospect of hell, and contrasting this with their own 'maximalist' approach, which seeks to initiate the believer into the richness of all that God has for those who seek salvation. However, such a portrayal is not totally fair, because like is not always being compared with like. If we were to compare popular Evangelicalism with popular Orthodoxy (a comparison which requires more study and explanation of their respective manifestations than has been possible here), we might find that a greater measure of similarity might be apparent, as would also be the case if we compared recognized spiritual writers within each tradition.

Perhaps the most poignant and fundamental difference between evangelical and Orthodox approaches to spirituality appears in the differing conceptions of the relationship between acceptance by God and spiritual growth: whereas evangelicals seek to grow in grace *because* they have been accepted, they perceive Orthodoxy as teaching that acceptance only comes at the end of this life and that persevering effort is necessary *in order* to be sure of acceptance. This is why such doctrines as justification by faith alone assume such significance in evangelical spirituality – because they are treated as providing a firm basis for such an outlook. The personal and pastoral importance of this difference makes further consideration a necessity, and this should include a careful attempt to relate the three tenses of salvation to one another. We could also express this theme in a way which shows that there is potential for fruitful discussion and possible convergence, by talking in terms of the relation between event and process in our respective understandings of salvation. Evangelicals would not deny that there is a process of sanctification which follows on from the event of justification, and the Orthodox would not deny that the process of *theosis* has its beginning at some point, whether that is baptism or (as must increasingly be the case in post-Christian societies) conversion.

## Notes

1 For an exploration of the parallels between Orthodoxy and Slavic Evangelicalism, see M. Elliott, 'Eastern Orthodox and Slavic Evangelicals: What Sets Them Both Apart From Western Evangelicals', *East-West Christian Ministry Report* 3 (Fall 1995), pp. 15–6.

2 Alister McGrath, *Evangelicalism and the Future of Christianity* (London: Hodder & Stoughton, 1993), p. 52.

3 Cf. the *Westminster Confession of Faith*, 11.2; in John H. Leith (ed.), *Creeds of the Churches* (Atlanta: John Knox, 1973), p. 207.

4 David K. Gillett, *Trust and Obey: Explorations in Evangelical Spirituality* (London: Darton, Longman & Todd, 1993), p. 2.

5 Metropolitan Anthony, *Living Prayer* (London: Darton, Longman & Todd, 1966), p. 66.

6 Kallistos Ware, *The Orthodox Way* (London: Mowbray, 1979), p. 149.

7 Kallistos Ware, *The Orthodox Church* (Harmondsworth: Pelican, 1997), pp. 258–9.

8 Ware, *Orthodox Way*, p. 14.

9  Ibid., p.28.

10  Ware, *Church*, pp. 21, 231–8.

11  Bishop Theophan the Recluse (1815–94), in Igumen Chariton, *The Art of Prayer: An Orthodox Anthology* (London: Faber & Faber, 1966), p. 236.

12  St John of Kronstadt (1829-1908), in G. P. Fedotov (ed.), *A Treasury of Russian Spirituality* (New York: Harper & Row, 1965), p. 366. Contemporary writers sometimes describe the Liturgy as 'tuning in' to the worship going on in heaven.

13  Ephrem Lash, *An Orthodox Prayer Book* (Oxford: Oxford University Press, 1999), p. xv.

14  Although the content of the many evangelical hymns and songs which are brief passages of Scripture or paraphrases of the biblical text may be seen as functioning in a similar way to the constant allusion to Scripture evident in Orthodox liturgical material.

15  Bishop Theophan, in Igumen Chariton, p. 99. Many evangelicals would question whether such practices can escape Jesus's critique of 'vain repetitions' (Mt. 6:7–8); in fairness, the repeated singing of a particular refrain (as sometimes happens in charismatic worship or that inspired by Taizé, for example) is also open to the same criticism.

16  Bishop Theophan, in Igumen Chariton, pp. 222, 224.

17  Metropolitan Anthony, pp. 53–4. Evangelicals would question this assertion, pointing to aspects of belief and practice which have changed, sometimes radically.

18  Vladimir Lossky, *The Mystical Theology of the Orthodox Church* (London: James Clarke, 1957), p. 7.

19  James M. Gordon, *Evangelical Spirituality* (London: SPCK, 1991), p. 6.

# 11

## Mission and evangelism

If evangelicals can be described as Bible people, they are also gospel people, with a message to share. Their presentation of this gospel will not, in a fair proportion of its doctrine and practice, be unfamiliar to Orthodox Christians, although its tone and style will to some extent be bewildering. Similarly, Orthodox missionary strategy at its most authentic is based on principles which are readily accepted by evangelicals. In this chapter, we will examine what mission means today, in practice as well as in theory, before concluding with some observations on how all this affects evangelical-Orthodox relations.

### i) Mission in theory

While Orthodox missiology has rarely been expressed in systematic form, its leading ideas may be ascertained by noting certain recurring features of Orthodox mission practice. These are rooted in an incarnational outlook:[1]

a) It has sought to use the vernacular language, even rendering it into writing where this has not previously been done. Continuing use by some jurisdictions of archaic languages such as church Slavonic for the Liturgy (which occupies such a significant position in Orthodox church life) has obscured this to some extent, but there are vigorous debates within Orthodoxy concerning liturgical language.

b) New converts have often been active in spreading the faith, but it has always been essential to see a church founded as soon as possible because of its importance as the sphere of salvation: the goal has thus been that of incorporation into the Church through the sacraments.

c) Clergy have been ordained as soon as possible from the indigenous population, with the longer-term objective of the church in a given area becoming self-governing.

d) The powerful witness provided by example has been recognized, as has that of the Liturgy itself, in which believers testify to their allegiance to a God who is transcendent over human life and history.

e) The ultimate purpose of mission is the revelation of the glory of God, a statement with which evangelicals will agree.

Evangelicals have discovered afresh in the latter half of the twentieth century that mission is more than just evangelism. Indeed, Andrew Kirk identifies five tasks for Christian mission:[2]

1. involvement in the stewardship in the resources of creation;
2. the service of human beings 'without distinction and whatever the need';
3. witness to Jesus Christ (Kirk includes apologetics and evangelism in this category);
4. the active engagement in seeing that God's justice is done in society;
5. a demonstration of what it means in practice to be a community of reconciliation and liberation.

Many evangelicals would accept that all these themes are vital to the *missio Dei*★. Indeed, evangelicals in the United Kingdom were, for much of the nineteenth century, at the forefront of asking questions about social justice; in recent decades they have begun to engage with such concerns again. The Evangelical Alliance has played a significant part in this in its establishment of groups like TEAR

Fund and the African & Caribbean Evangelical Alliance. There are now numerous evangelical churches and agencies addressing each of the above five themes. However, it should be said that for very many evangelicals, bearing witness to Christ is the central and essential point of mission and missionary activity, and that many would find it difficult to distinguish between evangelism and mission.

While evangelical missiologists such as Andrew Kirk, John Drane, and David Bosch would describe the driving force of evangelical mission as springing from the very being of God, for popular Evangelicalism the driving force for mission comes largely from a concern for the salvation of others. We shall return to this as the chapter proceeds, as it may prove pivotal in discerning the way forward for evangelical–Orthodox relations.

At a theological level, though, evangelical theologians have been rediscovering the fact that mission lies at the very heart of God's being, as seen supremely in the incarnation. Indeed, Kirk talks not so much of *missio Dei* for Christians, but of a *missio Trinitatis* or 'mission of the Trinity'; in his view, the 'mission of God flows directly from the nature of who God is'.[3] Human experience of community in some way reflects the nature of God as Trinity. The Orthodox may find much that resonates with this evangelical rediscovery.

If mission flows directly from the nature of God in this way, Bosch is correct to comment that as a task it is 'as coherent, broad and deep as the need and exigencies of human life'.[4] Evangelical theology of mission today encompasses more than just evangelistic proclamation, but includes much of what traditionally would have been called 'good works' or the 'social gospel'. This touches on what is perhaps the most difficult topic to work through, the relationship between mission and evangelism.

Evangelism is the setting in which most encounters between evangelicals and Orthodox Christians take place, especially in Eastern Europe. For evangelicals, evangelism is the proclamation of the good news of Jesus Christ. It involves an opportunity to respond personally and individually to the demands of Christ. Put starkly, for evangelicals the world is divided into two groups, those who know Christ and those who do not. There is an imperative on those who believe they have a relationship with Jesus to take this message to those who do not. This will include, for many evangelicals in Britain, people living in their street who do not attend church, even if they were once baptized as infants, for example in the Church of England or Church of Scotland. This may be difficult for the Orthodox to comprehend, given the Orthodox belief in baptism as a saving sacrament, although they will certainly identify with evangelical concern about the great numbers for whom baptism has not resulted in continuing involvement in the church. For many contemporary British evangelicals, conversion rather than baptism is the entry point into the church. Conversion does not happen at baptism, according to most evangelical traditions. This often means that evangelicals have difficulty in regarding baptized Orthodox as Christians. This springs not only from an evangelical emphasis on coming to personal faith in Christ but also, to some extent, from ignorance and misperception; the Orthodox too have provision for admission to the church upon confession of faith.

Such misperception makes serious conversation between the two communities difficult, and points up the divergence between Orthodox and evangelical ecclesiologies, the Orthodox Church being primarily territorial and evangelical churches largely 'gathered' congregations of those who choose to commit themselves to belong (although Britain and North America are seeing the emergence of new Orthodox congregations which are, in practice, 'gathered' churches composed largely of converts). The Orthodox regard the hierarchy of a given territory as possessing 'canonical jurisdiction' over it: the presence of more than one Orthodox jurisdiction in one area is regarded as an anomaly; much heart-searching has thus gone on among the Orthodox in the West where there is a plurality of jurisdictions. Furthermore, if there is an Orthodox Church in that area, many Orthodox would regard the arrival of any other church as an unwarranted and unwanted intrusion. It is difficult for evangelicals to grasp the consequent link between Orthodoxy and ethnic identity:[5] here the Orthodox have to strike a balance between recognizing their church's legitimate role as guardian of local culture, often in the face of Turkish or Communist opposition, and the heresy of *phyletism*, the identification of Christianity with a certain nationalist outlook. This error came to prominence during the nineteenth century, when political turbulence and nationalist aspirations affected much of Orthodox Europe. Another relevant factor is the Orthodox belief that baptism is a sacrament which all Christians share in common: thus many jurisdictions do not rebaptize converts from Protestantism or Roman Catholicism. The Orthodox may feel that evangelical mission in Orthodox areas represents a sectarian refusal to recognize the significance of baptism, a problem complicated by the fact that many evangelical missionaries would not accept infant baptism anyway.

It is important for the Orthodox, who make a close connection between soteriology, ecclesiology and mission, to understand that for evangelicals evangelism is not always undertaken directly by a particular church. Evangelism in other countries undertaken by Christians from the United Kingdom is primarily done under the auspices of missionary agencies, although increasingly the local church works in partnership with the agency. Evangelists and missionaries encountered by Orthodox Christians may not be tied in to any ecclesiastical structure. This is extremely rare within Orthodoxy, something that evangelicals would do well to note. When encountered in the polemical crucible, evangelical witness can, because of such individualism, appear to the Orthodox as alien as Orthodox worship appears to the average evangelical.

There has been an increasing emphasis on evangelism by evangelicals in Orthodox countries following the collapse of the Eastern bloc and as they worked towards the year 2000. Chief amongst the strategies adopted have been *Dawn 2000*\* and the emphasis on the '10/40 window'\*. Such activity results again, in part, from the impression among evangelicals that the Orthodox have not heard the message of Christ. This is something to which we will return below.


## ii) Mission in practice

How does the above work out in practice? In this report, convergences and differences in doctrinal belief and in practice have emerged. There are other areas, perhaps in social justice or personal ethics, where evangelicals and Orthodox will be able to stand shoulder to shoulder. But how does an evangelical understand an Orthodox Christian, and vice versa?

Many British evangelicals will interpret Orthodoxy in the light of their experiences of Roman Catholicism or Anglo-Catholicism (an understandable approach based on external appearances, although Orthodoxy differs from Roman Catholicism in many respects). The ritual will appear alien, irrelevant and, more importantly, seem 'dead'. Many evangelicals regard Orthodoxy, like Roman Catholicism, as being in error in its teaching about how we are saved. For these reasons they tend to assume that the Orthodox are among those who need to hear the good news of Christ. They may come to this conclusion with very little knowledge of Orthodoxy, except perhaps a belief that it is primarily an ethnic phenomenon. To complicate things, evangelicals may recollect that Orthodoxy has often relied in its mission upon governmental privileges and assistance. Contemporary Orthodox mission activity in Asia and Africa will probably be unknown, as may the story of the persecution of the Orthodox under Communism. Some evangelicals will have heard rumours of others converting to Orthodoxy, but be bewildered as to why.

The Orthodox likewise will have little understanding of Evangelicalism. They would naturally be bewildered by its understanding of the Church and its lack of appeal to Tradition and the saints. The question of the individual evangelical's status would perhaps not be an issue as the Orthodox do not generally think of salvation in individualistic terms, although in Eastern Europe Orthodox priests are known to warn local people of the personal dangers of leaving Orthodoxy.

What happens when a British evangelical takes presuppositions on to the mission field? Or when an Orthodox engages in Orthodox-evangelical conversation in the United Kingdom? Much depends on the view of the individual evangelical or missionary agency. For evangelicals there is the ever-present desire to safeguard a pure doctrinal position; for the Orthodox there is a concern lest something foreign or heretical infiltrate their communities. This in many ways sums up evangelical mission in Orthodox lands: evangelicals often doubt whether Orthodox doctrine and spirituality are 'sound', while Orthodox frequently perceive Evangelicalism as Western and therefore unwelcome, particularly in countries which are going through a period of searching for new identities. To complicate things, each will find that the actual manifestation of the other tradition is not monochrome at all but will often differ significantly from what they have learned about it in their reading or from official teaching and policy. Not only so, but what evangelicals or Orthodox say today may not always be quite what they were saying in generations past; thus conservatives on each side criticize contemporary representatives of their own faith for perceived compromise, whether they express this in terms of the need to remain faithful to Tradition or in terms of the need to proclaim the same message as the Reformers and the eighteenth-century leaders.

Is this impasse resolvable? There are perhaps two reasons to hope that it is: Orthodox recognition that it needs to adjust itself to the post-Communist era, and Evangelicalism's own struggles with culture. Both Orthodox and evangelical are thus aware of the need for the gospel to be relevant to culture without being captive to it. The Orthodox are only too aware of their re-emergence into a new era following the collapse of Communism. Ion Bria notes that under Communism, Orthodoxy had become a 'religious institution' rather than a 'missionary movement'.[6] Bria calls for a rediscovery of mission: 'The gospel has to be proclaimed and taught in every generation, *in its own language and symbols*. It cannot be appropriated once for all by a particular culture; it has to be liberated for new connections and new praxis.'[7] This should resonate with those of us who live in the West, where Christianity is being forced to think of fresh ways in which the gospel can be made meaningful for a postmodern audience. Evangelicals should welcome these sentiments and take to heart Bria's criticism that their evangelistic strategies do not engage with the culture of Eastern European countries, but rather create a Christianity which is disjoined from the heritage of places like Romania, Serbia and Russia. However, they will also wish to join their Eastern brethren in calling upon regional Orthodox jurisdictions to resist the temptation to return to the pattern of state-church relationships which obtained in the pre-Communist era.

The shared experience of the struggle to relate the gospel to contemporary culture should in itself engender hope for a more fruitful interchange between evangelicals and Orthodox Christians.[8] As both struggle to make the gospel intelligible to their respective communities, it may be that much can be learned from each other. In Eastern Europe, the most significant attempts so far in this respect have been in Romania,[9] although even there both constituencies have faced stern opposition from their co-religionists.


## iii) Evangelism

There is no real consensus concerning how to proceed in terms of missionary activities in Orthodox countries by evangelical agencies. Individuals may work alongside, indeed under, the authority of an Orthodox priest; some agencies are happy to employ Orthodox Christians in their work. Going beyond this, one missionary organisation with the expressed wish to work with Orthodox structures is the Servant of Servants Foundation, based in the United States. Their vision is set out in David Bjork's *Unfamiliar Paths*.[10] Bjork's intention is to work within the structures of Orthodox churches, seeking to encourage discipleship *within* them, rather than wanting to rescue Orthodox Christians *from* them.[11] Similarly, Billy Graham has been happy, when ministering in Orthodox countries, to encourage follow-up to his evangelistic missions to be undertaken by Orthodox clergy within their parish structures. This is but a particular application of his general approach, which allows him to work alongside churches of a variety of theological opinions; if a church wishes to support his mission, he is happy to refer inquirers to them. A number of other examples could be quoted of co-operation (especially in Russia) between evangelicals and Orthodox in the fields of care of the needy, education, Bible distribution and literature production.

British missionary societies appear to be more ambivalent as to what approach to take with Orthodox people. This is not in itself surprising, given the tendency of the evangelical constituency within Britain to see the Orthodox as legitimate targets for mission. This is an especially delicate issue in view of the fact that, notwithstanding some recent withdrawals or suspensions of membership, most Orthodox jurisdictions are fellow-members of the World Council of Churches alongside some of the very Protestant traditions who are engaging in outreach which is at times spiritually and culturally insensitive. Many other individual evangelical churches in the West support mission work in Orthodox countries. However, it is possible that in local situations, there is a greater degree of conversation and understanding.

Many evangelicals in the United Kingdom, as they begin to appreciate Orthodoxy, are able to recognize many committed Orthodox as fellow believers, and there are Orthodox who readily recognize within Evangelicalism brothers and sisters in Christ. Such growth in relationships is a hopeful sign, though it may require a period of reflection before fresh approaches and partnerships in the gospel emerge. It is also much less common in Eastern Europe.

In the light of all this, one fundamental question may be posed to intending mission agencies and sending churches about a proposed new area of operation: where, or perhaps what, is the existing church in that situation, and what relationships need to be established with it?

## Notes

1 This paragraph is based largely upon James J. Stamoolis, *Eastern Orthodox Mission Theology Today* (Maryknoll, NY: Orbis, 1986).

2 J. Andrew Kirk, 'Missiology', in Sinclair B. Ferguson and David F. Wright (eds.), *New Dictionary of Theology* (Leicester: IVP, 1988), p. 435.

3 J. Andrew Kirk, *What is Mission? Theological Explorations* (London: Darton, Longman & Todd, 1999), p. 27.

4 David Bosch, *Transforming Mission* (Maryknoll, NY: Orbis, 1988), p. 173.

5 Interestingly, some Orthodox have attempted to make a link between

Orthodoxy and Englishness, e.g. Andrew, Philips, *Orthodox Christianity and the English Tradition* (Felixstowe, Suffolk: English Orthodox Trust, 1995).

6 Ion Bria, *The Liturgy after the Liturgy* (Geneva: World Council of Churches, 1996), p. 46.

7 Ibid., p. 49.

8 See further B. Hoedemaker, *Secularization and Mission: A Theological Essay* (Leominster: Gracewing, 1998).

9 See, for example, Paul Botica, 'Kissing the Crucifix: Practical Steps toward Effective Ecumenical Dialogue and Cooperation in Romania', *Religion in Eastern Europe* 19.2 (April 1999), pp. 21–43; and note the ongoing work of the evangelical-sponsored Areopagus project in Timişoara.

10 David Bjork, *Unfamiliar Paths* (Pasadena, CA: William Carey Library, 1997).

11 For a nineteenth-century parallel to this, see 'David Edwards', '200 Years of Missions to Muslims. Part 2: The First Century', *Centre for Islamic Studies Newsletter* 7 (Winter 1999), pp. 8–9. The author outlines and evaluates the approach adopted by Claudius Buchanan and other nineteenth-century evangelicals, who saw the renewal of indigenous Orthodox churches as crucial to the success of outreach among Muslims.

# 12

## Conclusions and recommendations

1. We rejoice at the extent of common ground which we have discovered in our discussions, and we encourage our respective constituencies to recognize and affirm those truths which we have in common. We note with gratitude the extent of doctrinal agreement between us in the areas of Scripture, the doctrine of God, the divine institution of the Church and its missionary task, the last things, the need for personal experience of God, and the normative status of Scripture for personal ethics. Together we uphold as non-negotiable the apostolic faith attested by the creeds of the early church.

2. If much of this common ground normally goes unrecognized, we should think about how we might give it visible expression in our relationships with one another; indeed, we should also consider how much those beliefs which we claim to uphold are given visible expression within the life and faith of our own communities. Shared insistence upon the uniqueness of Jesus Christ as the incarnate Son of God and shared concern to distance ourselves from syncretism or relativism may help to impart a sense of perspective to discussion of those issues which still divide us.

3. Nevertheless, we acknowledge that deep theological differences remain between the evangelical and Orthodox communities, notably in the area of our understandings of salvation, of the

Church, and of the relationship between Scripture and Tradition; other differences involve patterns of worship and ministry, and beliefs concerning the sacraments. There is also great potential for misunderstanding arising out of our use of theological terminology: we may use the same terms but attach different meanings to them. We have different ways of doing theology, and different philosophical frameworks which help to shape our theology. Further encounter and conversation must recognize this dimension, and from the start we shall need to pay attention to defining our worldviews as well as our terminology. Evangelicals and Orthodox members of this study group agree that differences must be taken seriously and discussions must not be unduly rushed. Hence we have not felt it right to consider the issue of intercommunion: other fundamental matters need to be dealt with first.

4. We believe that contact between evangelical and Orthodox communities has considerable potential, not least because encountering another tradition stimulates us to reflect critically and appreciatively on our own theology and sense of identity. Two comments about underlying presuppositions may be in order, however. *First*, involvement in such conversations should not be taken as implying that either side accepts the other's form of the Christian faith as being of equal validity; there will be many things which we feel we can learn from our counterparts, but there will also remain issues on which we cannot accept their teaching. *Second*, both communities would need to agree that encounter between two Christian traditions represents contact of a different order from that involved in the encounter between Christianity and a non-Christian religious tradition.

There is a need for clarification of what is meant by 'ecumenism'. Many on both sides regard it as a pejorative term and are suspicious of any activity which is thus designated; behind this may lie concerns about matters such as political manipulation or doctrinal and ethical compromise, or else a lack of experience of, or interest in, contact with believers of other Christian traditions. A distinction needs to be made between the kind of contact envisaged here, between communities which 'confess Jesus Christ as God and

Saviour according to the Scriptures',[1] and that which denies the uniqueness of Jesus Christ by an acceptance of all religions as paths to salvation. This is not to deny the real value of inter-religious discussion and understanding, but such contact is not of the same order, nor does it have the same goals.

5. Evangelical–Orthodox encounter carries with it the possibility that participants may decide to convert from one of these forms of the Christian faith to the other. Evangelicals and Orthodox should consider how they would react to such an outcome. They should also reflect on the issues which may lead individuals to make such a decision.

6. In establishing an appropriate methodology for continuing conversations, it should be recognized that in order to appeal to evangelicals the Orthodox must engage in rigorous study of the Scriptures, while evangelicals must steep themselves in the teaching of the Fathers and the early councils if they are to present a case which the Orthodox will find acceptable.

7. Further joint study of the Scriptures is urgently needed and active steps should be taken to make this a reality. Such study is, however, complicated by the need for each side to become acquainted with unfamiliar ways of reading and studying the text. Evangelicals will need to familiarize themselves with the Orthodox approach which insists upon the need to read Scripture in the light of Tradition, and the frequent use of such devices as allegory to bring out the Christocentric nature of Scripture, while the Orthodox will need to develop a sympathetic understanding of the evangelical insistence upon the individual's direct access (aided by the Spirit) to the meaning of Scripture, coupled with the utilization of historical-critical methods of exegesis.

8. In studying the Scriptures together, we should acknowledge the distorted perceptions which we often have of one another's attitudes to the Bible. Evangelicals will need to take more seriously the place that Scripture has in Orthodox worship and discipleship,

and to give due weight to St Paul's teaching and practice concerning the 'tradition'. The Orthodox must reckon with the various checks and balances in Evangelicalism that prevent personal access to the Scriptures from degenerating into individualism. We urge evangelicals to appreciate the Scriptures as God's gift *to* the Church, *through* the Church; this would foster a stronger communal dimension to evangelical study and teaching of the Scriptures. We urge the Orthodox to recognize the freedom of God's written word in directly addressing, rebuking and correcting – as well as nourishing – the Church of Christ, and to give stronger support to the practice of personal and family Bible reading.

9. The creeds and definitions of the early centuries have shaped the belief of all Christian traditions, Protestant and Catholic as well as Orthodox. Since, as we have seen, the early Fathers have been appealed to by Protestants as well as the Orthodox, and may fairly be regarded as the possession of the whole church, East and West, we believe that joint study of their writings is needed. This could be a fruitful way of establishing common doctrinal foundations. In such a context, it will be possible to examine the fundamental issues of belief raised by the *Filioque* clause in the Western form of the Nicene Creed. Furthermore, involvement of Roman Catholics in this, as in other aspects of Orthodox-evangelical dialogue, is something which we recognize as highly desirable. This three-way co-operation is already evident in projects such as the *Ancient Christian Commentaries* series, which is producing biblical commentaries compiled from patristic writings.[2] Orthodoxy and Evangelicalism have both separated from Rome, although at different times and for different reasons. For Orthodoxy, any reconciliation with evangelicals is most likely to come about as part of a renewal of sympathetic understanding of the Western theological tradition as a whole; for evangelicals, many of the issues raised by contact with Orthodoxy are also raised by contact with Roman Catholicism. We must therefore resist the temptation to seek common ground between Orthodoxy and Evangelicalism in what may be called 'counter-Catholicism'.

10. We recommend that contact between Evangelicalism and the Orthodox Churches in the United Kingdom be continued at the highest levels possible. Some form of officially-sponsored conversation would be potentially the most fruitful, and we would like to see exploratory talks undertaken with a minimum of delay. These will need to establish the basis upon which such conversation could take place and its specific objectives. We note that recent Orthodox-Reformed dialogue has focused on joint study of successive articles of the Nicene Creed; this may be one agenda which could be followed. Another possibly fruitful line of investigation lies in the recent emphasis in ecumenical circles on the idea of the Church as *koinonia*; consideration of the relationship between our life together and the life of the Trinity would raise many pertinent issues for joint deliberation.

11. Contact at the local level is also desirable. We recognize the need for leaders to encourage the evangelical and Orthodox traditions to change their perceptions of each other at this level, and notably to challenge the widespread belief that all members of the other tradition may be dismissed out of hand as 'unsaved' or 'heretics'. To that end, we suggest that members of each community seek out local representatives or congregations of the other, develop personal relationships and if possible attend their services. Such 'grass roots' contact is especially important because these traditions are not theological abstractions but represent the lived faith of millions of people. Our encounter must be with Evangelicalism and Orthodoxy as they are lived out in practice, not merely with one another's liturgical books and theological writings.

12. We are aware that in certain areas of the world there are considerable tensions between evangelicals and the Orthodox. We pray for a greater level of mutual understanding between the two communities, and to that end we encourage those working in such situations actively to seek out and build relationships with their counterparts as far as possible. Such contact is particularly vital at the local level. Much work urgently requires to be done for the healing of wounds caused by past insensitivity and ignorance on

both sides. This will include open acknowledgement of those injustices and hurts which each side believes it has suffered at the hands of the other, with a view to seeking resolution and reconciliation, as well as consideration of the relationship between (a) Orthodoxy, ethnicity, religious establishment and national identity; and (b) Evangelicalism and Western culture.

13. The relationship between gospel and culture is one topic which there has not been room to cover in this report, and which needs to be examined by evangelicals and Orthodox together. There have been initiatives in this field which have sought to draw together Christians from various traditions, and we believe that such work is worthy of a higher profile in our communities. It would also be valuable to consider from a historical perspective how different cultures have helped to shape, or been shaped by, each tradition's understanding of the gospel.

14. Evangelical churches which send out missionaries should formulate a mission policy which recognizes the importance of informed understanding of the local religious context, and of seeking to establish good relationships with local Christians and churches of all traditions. For this to be done, there is a need for widespread dissemination of relevant information; mission agencies can play a key role in this.

15. We encourage denominations and mission agencies with an interest in work in Orthodox countries to set up forums for discussion and assessment of possible mission strategies. Bodies which bring together these agencies, such as Global Connections, are well placed to play a valuable role in facilitating this process, and we urge agencies to avail themselves of the services of such bodies.

16. We suggest that theological courses in each constituency include some element of introduction to the other's history, beliefs and practices. This could be achieved through specific courses (as is already the case in some Eastern European institutions) but also by teaching in other fields, such as church history or the history of

doctrine, which takes into account the perspectives and writings of scholars from the other constituency.

17. A related and equally important area is that of the relationship between church and state. In the rapidly secularizing Western world, historical church-state links are being eroded and those which remain are seen increasingly as problematic; many evangelicals would, in any case, advocate a clear separation between church and state. However, in Eastern Europe, it appears that Orthodox hierarchies are often keen to recover privileged relationships with the authorities akin to those which existed before the spread of Communism. There is evidence to justify evangelicals in these countries in the conviction that this is leading to discrimination against them. If the Orthodox in the United Kingdom were able to demonstrate an active sympathy with evangelical concerns, this would do much to improve relationships.

18. More generally, evangelicals and Orthodox could investigate the possibilities for co-operation in such fields as ethical education and influencing the course of public policy. In view of their shared desire to uphold ethical principles based on the teaching of Scripture, it would seem likely that this could be a very fruitful and rewarding area in which to work, not only in terms of improved relationships between the two communities, but more particularly in terms of being able to witness together to belief in a God who desires to enter into relationship with human beings. Care must be taken, however, that this does not become an opportunity for a covert agenda which encourages the practice of proselytism under cover of co-operative activity. This is not to be taken as denying the legitimacy of evangelism, but as expressing the belief that evangelistic testimony is to be carried on in an honourable and truthful manner.

19. All the above must take into account that evangelicals and Orthodox are already encountering each other daily, especially in Eastern Europe, and that the nature of the relationships and impressions thus formed will affect what can be achieved in the

future.[3] Thus even the most theoretical-sounding of these recommendations have practical import: what we will be able to do will be constrained or facilitated by the climate which our dialogue (or lack of it) helps to create. All the talking (and there will need to be more of it than we might initially accept) is to serve the aim of knowing Christ better ourselves and making him known more faithfully to a world which needs him.

## Notes

1 This phrase is taken from the constitutional Basis of the World Council of Churches.

2 This series is edited by Thomas Oden, and published by IVP in the United States.

3 For an example of what constitutes good practice, see Anita Deyneka, 'Guidelines for Foreign Missionaries in the Former Soviet Union', in John Witte, Jr and Michael Bourdeaux (eds), *Proselytism and Orthodoxy in Russia* (Maryknoll, NY: Orbis, 1999), pp. 331–40.

# Appendix: The Ecumenical Councils

The following seven councils are accepted as 'ecumenical' (from the Greek *oikumene*, 'the inhabited world') because it was claimed that their decisions secured universal acceptance. However, at most of them the church in the Western half of the Roman Empire was poorly represented, and it is evident from history that the decisions of these councils often provoked further disagreement rather than ending it. Rome regards a number of later councils as ecumenical, but these are not accepted as such by Protestants or Orthodox. Evangelicals usually have few problems in assenting to the doctrinal decisions of the first four councils, and some also accept those of the fifth and sixth.

## 1. Nicea (325)

Nicea affirmed Christ's full deity against those who taught that he was a created being of an inferior order to the Father. It produced the 'Creed of Nicea', which described him as being 'of one essence with the Father'. However, this was understood in various ways, leading to fierce controversy.

## 2. Constantinople (381)

Some who upheld the divinity of Christ were doing so in a way that appeared to deny his full humanity, denying that he possessed a human soul. This council condemned those who in effect were denying the full humanity of Christ, reaffirming and clarifying the teaching of Nicea: Christ must be fully human or he could not redeem humanity. In guarded terms, it also upheld belief in the divinity of the Holy Spirit. Only later was the Nicene or Niceno-Constantinopolitan Creed ascribed to this council.

### 3. Ephesus (431)

At Ephesus the unity of the divine and human natures in Christ's Person was affirmed in the face of teaching which appeared to separate the divine Christ from the human Jesus. Here the description of Mary as *theotokos* ('God-bearer') was upheld as orthodox because of its importance for Christology.

### 4. Chalcedon (451)

The most significant doctrinal definition of the early centuries was that produced at Chalcedon. Building on the Creed of Nicea, as well as the Nicene Creed, the 'Chalcedonian Definition' set bounds to orthodox understanding of the Person of Christ. His divine and human natures were declared to subsist in one Person 'without confusion, without change, without division, without separation'.

### 5. Constantinople II (553)

In an attempt to conciliate those who felt that Chalcedon had not done enough to assert the unity of Christ's Person, this council declared that Christ's human nature received its personal identity as a result of its union with his divine Person. It also declared that Mary remained permanently a virgin (a doctrine which Protestant Reformers such as Luther and Calvin were happy to accept).

### 6. Constantinople III (680–1)

This council asserted that if Christ is fully human and fully divine, he must therefore have a human will as well as a divine will.

## 7. Nicea II (787)

The most problematic of the councils for evangelicals, Nicea II affirmed the legitimacy of the production of icons, as well as encouraging their veneration in the setting of the church's worship. In response to those who claimed that making icons broke the biblical prohibitions on making 'graven images', the council justified them on the ground that Christ had become incarnate and therefore representations of him as human could be made. Veneration could be given to icons as it was to other symbols, such as the cross; such honour was seen as passing to Christ whom these material symbols represented.

# Suggestions for further reading

## Orthodoxy

NB: Some of these titles may be difficult to obtain; if you cannot order them through your usual sources, the following operate a mail-order service for Orthodox books:

Orthodox Christian Books Ltd, 7 Townhouse Farm, Alsager Rd, Audley, Staffs, ST7 8JQ (Tel: 07000 790330)

Russian Orthodox Cathedral Bookshop, Cathedral of the Dormition and All Saints, 67 Ennismore Gdns, London, SW7 1NH (0207 722 2879)

St George Orthodox Information Service, The White House, Mettingham, Bungay, Suffolk, NR35 1TP (01986 896708)

*Introductory / General*

Bulgakov, Sergius, *The Orthodox Church* (Crestwood, NY: St Vladimir's Seminary Press, 1988)

*Christian History* magazine, especially nos. 18 ('The Millennium of Russian Christianity'), 44 ('John Chrysostom'), 51 ('Heresy in the Early Church') and 54 ('Eastern Orthodoxy')

Available from larger bookshops; published by *Christianity Today*.

Coniaris, Anthony M., *Introducing the Orthodox Church: Its Faith and Life* (Minneapolis: Light & Life, 1982)

*Evangel* 17:1 (Spring 1999)

On Orthodoxy and Evangelicalism in the United Kingdom; basic coverage, intended for evangelical pastors. Available from Paternoster Periodicals, PO Box 300, Carlisle, Cumbria, CA3 0QR.

Fairbairn, Don, 'Partakers of the Divine Nature: An Introduction to Eastern Orthodox Theology' (revised 1996), available from Global Center, Beeson Divinity School, Samford University, 800 Lakeshore Drive, Birmingham, AL 35229, USA. Assessment by an evangelical who has taught extensively in Ukraine.

Parry, Ken *et al.* (eds), *The Blackwell Dictionary of Eastern Christianity* (Oxford: Blackwell, 1999)

Robertson, Jenny, *Windows to Eternity: A personal exploration of Russian Orthodoxy* (Oxford: Bible Reading Fellowship, 1999)

Ware, Timothy [Kallistos], *The Orthodox Church* (Harmondsworth: Pelican, 1997, revised)

### History

Schmemann, Alexander, *The Historical Road of Eastern Orthodoxy* (London: Harvill, 1963)

### Theology

St Athanasius, *On the Incarnation of the Word of God*

St Basil the Great, *On the Holy Spirit*

St John of Damascus, *On the Divine Images*

These (and other writings by some of the Fathers) are available in modern translations, published by Cassell (London). Though listed here, the Fathers should be seen as part of the heritage of the whole church, not of Orthodoxy alone.

Bria, Ion, *The Liturgy after the Liturgy: Mission and Witness from an Orthodox Perspective* (Geneva: World Council of Churches, 1996)

Keshishian, Aram, *Orthodox Perspectives on Mission* (Oxford: Regnum/Lynx, 1992)

Lossky, Vladimir, *The Mystical Theology of the Orthodox Church* (London: James Clarke, 1957)

Can be hard going, but well worth it as an excellent introduction to Orthodox theology.

Saucy, Robert L., John Coe and Alan W. Gomes, 'Task Force

Report: Eastern Orthodox Teachings in Comparison with The Doctrinal Position of Biola University', 1998 (available from http://people.biola.edu/faculty/alanG/EO/EO.htm).

Biola University is an evangelical institution in the United States, several of whose faculty members converted to Orthodoxy.

Stamoolis, James J., *Eastern Orthodox Mission Theology Today* (Maryknoll, NY: Orbis, 1986)

Ware, Kallistos, *How are we Saved?* (Minneapolis, MN: Light & Life, 1996)

——————, *The Orthodox Way* (Crestwood, NY: St Vladimir's Seminary Press, 1995, revised)

*Worship and Spirituality*

The best place to start is with a copy of the Liturgy of St John Chrysostom, which is used for most Sundays. Available in a variety of translations, an easily obtainable modern one is: *The Divine Liturgy of Our Father among the Saints John Chrysostom* (Oxford: Oxford University Press, 1995), with parallel English and Greek text.

There are many other liturgical services in the Orthodox Church; a wide selection may be found in: Hapgood, Isobel F., *The Service book of the Orthodox Church* (Oxford: Oxford University Press, 1922). A more recent edition was published by the Antiochian Archdiocese of North America.

Chariton, Igumen, *The Art of Prayer: An Orthodox Anthology* (London: Faber & Faber, 1966)

French, R. M. (tr.), *The Way of a Pilgrim* (London: Triangle/SPCK, 1995²). A classic work of Russian spirituality, focusing on the use of the 'Jesus Prayer'.

A number of volumes of the *Philokalia* have appeared in English, published by Faber & Faber (London).

Seddon, Deborah, *Gospel Icons* (Cambridge: Grove, 1999).

Brief illustrated introduction by an evangelical.

*Conversions*

Gillquist, Peter, *Becoming Orthodox: A Journey to the Ancient Christian Faith* (Ben Lomond, CA: Conciliar Press, 1992, revised)

Harper, Michael, *A Faith Fulfilled* (Ben Lomond, CA: Conciliar Press, 1999); published earlier as *The True Light* (London: Hodder & Stoughton, 1997).

A prominent Anglican evangelical's journey into Orthodoxy.

Schaeffer, Frank, *Dancing Alone: The Quest for the Orthodox Faith in the Age of False Religion* (Brookline, MA: Holy Cross Orthodox Press, 1994).

Frank is the son of the evangelical apologist and thinker Francis Schaeffer.

## Evangelicalism

*Introductory / General*

ACUTE, *What is an Evangelical?* (London: Evangelical Alliance, 1997)

Calver, Clive & Rob Warner, *Together We Stand: Evangelical Convictions, Unity and Vision* (London: Hodder & Stoughton, 1996)

McGrath, Alister, *Evangelicalism and the Future of Christianity* (London: Hodder & Stoughton, 1993)

Stott, John R. W., *Basic Christianity* (Leicester: IVP, first published 1958).

Classic presentation of the evangelical understanding of the gospel.

Tidball, Derek J., *Who are the Evangelicals? Tracing the roots of the modern movements* (Basingstoke: Marshall Pickering, 1994)

Whale, J. S., *The Protestant Tradition* (Cambridge: Cambridge University Press, 1960)

*History*

Barclay, Oliver, *Evangelicalism in Britain 1935–1995* (Leicester: IVP, 1997)

Bebbington, D. W., *Evangelicalism in Modern Britain: A history from the 1730s to the 1980s* (London: Unwin Hyman, 1989)

Noll, Mark A., George Rawlyk and David Bebbington, *Evangelicalism* (New York: OUP, 1994)

*Theology*

Calvin, John (ed. J. T. McNeill, tr. F. L. Battles), *Institutes of the Christian Religion* (London: SCM / Philadelphia, PA: Westminster, 1960).

Ferguson, Sinclair B. and David F. Wright (eds), *New Dictionary of Theology* (Leicester: IVP, 1988)

George, Timothy, *Theology of the Reformers* (Leicester: Apollos, 1988)

Grudem, Wayne, *Systematic Theology: An Introduction to Christian Doctrine* (Leicester: IVP, 1994)

McGrath, Alister E., *A Passion for Truth: The Intellectual Coherence of Evangelicalism* (Leicester: Apollos, 1996)

Milne, Bruce, *Know the Truth* (Leicester: IVP, 1998)

Stott, John, *The Cross of Christ* (Leicester: IVP, 1986)
Expounds a doctrine which is at the heart of evangelical belief.

Outler, Albert C. & Richard P. Heitzenrater (eds), *John Wesley's Sermons: An Anthology* (Nashville, TN: Abingdon, 1991)

*Worship & Spirituality*

Bunyan, John, *Pilgrim's Progress* (available in many modern editions).

Gillett, David K., *Trust and Obey: Explorations in Evangelical Spirituality* (London: Darton, Longman & Todd, 1993)

Gordon, James M., *Evangelical Spirituality* (London: SPCK, 1991)

Packer, J. I., *Knowing God* (London: Hodder & Stoughton, 1973)

*Ethics*

Atkinson, D. J. (ed.), *New Dictionary of Christian Ethics and Pastoral Theology* (Leicester: IVP, 1995)

Stott, John R. W., *The Contemporary Christian* (Leicester: IVP, 1995)
Formerly published as *Issues Facing Christians Today*.

## Joint Dialogues and Consultations

*Anglican-Orthodox Dialogue: The Dublin Agreed Statement* (London: SPCK, 1984)

van Beek, Huibert and Georges Lemopoulos (eds), *Proclaiming Christ Today: Orthodox – Evangelical Consultation, Alexandria, 10–15 July 1995* (Geneva/Bialystok: World Council of Churches/Syndesmos, 1995) van Beek, Huibert and Georges Lemopoulos (eds), *Turn To God, Rejoice in Hope: Orthodox – Evangelical Consultation, Hamburg, 30 March–4 April, 1998* (Geneva: World Council of Churches, 1998)

*Christian Witness to Nominal Christians Among the Orthodox*, Lausanne Committee for World Evangelization Occasional Paper no. 19 (London: Scripture Union, 1980)

Colson, Charles and Richard Neuhaus, *Evangelicals and Catholics Together* (Dallas, TX: Word/London: Hodder & Stoughton, 1995/1996)

Cutsinger, James (ed.), *Reclaiming the Great Tradition: Evangelicals, Catholics, and Orthodox in Dialogue* (Downers Grove, IL: IVP, 1997)

Torrance, Thomas F. (ed.), *Theological Dialogue between Orthodox and Reformed Churches*, 2 vols. (Edinburgh: Scottish Academic Press, 1985, 1993)

Demanding; Reformed participants are more 'orthodox' than specifically evangelical.

Teague, David P. (ed.), *Turning Over a New Leaf: Protestant Missions and the Orthodox Churches of the Middle East* (London: Interserve, 1992[2])

Deals as much with the Oriental Orthodox as with the Eastern or Chalcedonian Orthodox.

Vischer, Lukas (ed.), *Agreed Statements From The Orthodox-Reformed Dialogue* (Geneva: World Alliance of Reformed Churches, 1998)

Ware, K and C. Davey (eds.), *Anglican-Orthodox Dialogue: The Moscow Agreed Statement* (London: SPCK, 1977)

# Glossary

**Chrismation**: the anointing with oil of the newly baptized and those received into Orthodoxy from other Christian communities, symbolizing the gift of the Holy Spirit, sometimes seen as comparable to the Western rite of Confirmation.

**'Dawn 2000'**: an evangelistic strategy, originally developed in the Philippines, which set out to 'Disciple A Whole Nation' by 2000 through planting a church in each local community: evangelical denominations and evangelistic agencies were to work together to achieve this, setting goals for the growth of their own organization but co-operating with others.

**Dispensationalism**: a species of evangelical thought which divides God's dealings with humanity into periods or dispensations. In each God lays down a particular way in which he desires humanity to respond to him, but each terminates in the failure of the mass to do so, giving rise to a new dispensation. Dispensationalists insist upon the literal fulfilment of prophecy; thus they see God's purposes as focusing on earthly Israel, with the Church (a body which is heavenly in its essential nature) as a parenthesis between the Old Testament era and the eschatological restoration of the Jews to the land of Israel. It should be distinguished from the expectations of an earthly millennium found in some early Fathers.

**Economy**: in this report, the word refers to God's saving purpose as manifest in human history. The term is also used by Orthodox to refer to occasions when the Church's normal rules may be set aside in particular instances for the sake of the salvation of those concerned: this may occur in areas as diverse as allowing non-Orthodox to take communion and the remarriage of divorced persons.

***Missio Dei***: 'the mission of God'; used by missiologists to emphasize that mission is primarily God's work, in which Christians are called to share.

***Pascha***: An early Christian and Orthodox term for Easter; it originally referred to the Jewish Passover.

**Puritanism**: this movement began in England during the second half of the sixteenth century, with the objective of purifying the Church of England from all unscriptural practices and making it more completely Reformed in its forms of worship and government. Whilst Puritan theology and spirituality belong within the Reformed tradition, seventeenth-century Puritans were noted exponents of an intense personal spirituality which was not shared by all Protestants.

**Pietism**: a movement which originated in German Lutheranism during the seventeenth century as a reaction against the perceived deadness of orthodox Protestantism. Pietists, like Puritans, sought to help people to a living relationship with God, but were less sympathetic than Puritans to post-Reformation developments in Protestant theology. Pietist influence was a major factor in the evangelical conversions of John and Charles Wesley, thus passing into English-speaking evangelicalism.

***Semper reformanda***: a phrase used soon after the Protestant Reformation to refer to the church's being 'always in need of, or open to, further reformation'.

***Sobornost***: a term first used of Orthodox ecclesiology by the Russian Orthodox thinker A. S. Khomiakov (1804-60) and popular in modern ecumenical discussion. Sometimes rendered in English as 'conciliarity', it refers to the way in which freedom and unity in Christ are harmonized in the Church through consultation.

***Sola scriptura***: literally 'Scripture alone'. Coined to express the Reformation insistence upon the supreme authority of Scripture as the judge in all matters of the church's faith and practice.

***Synergism***: literally 'working together'. It refers to the Orthodox belief that human beings, while sinful, are nevertheless capable of co-operating with God. Thus divine grace is not seen as excluding human freedom, choice and ability. However, the Orthodox deny that we can earn or merit grace by our co-operation. Similar beliefs are also found in Protestantism, although they are not always developed in the same way.

**'10/40 window'**: the countries between latitudes 10°N and 40°N, seen by some evangelical mission strategists as in particular need of missionary outreach.

*Theosis*: often translated as 'deification' or 'divinization'. Orthodox believe that we participate in the divine nature through the process of salvation (cf. 2 Pet. 1:3–4). Deification may be understood as the combination of sanctification and glorification (for a fuller explanation, see Ch. 10).

*Theotokos*: used of the Virgin Mary, and often rendered as 'Mother of God'. The term became prominent during the fifth-century disputes about the Person of Christ, and was intended to assert that the child born of Mary was, from the moment of conception, none other than the incarnate Son of God, not a mere human being who was 'adopted' as the Son of God, or had divinity conferred upon him, at a later point (such as his baptism). The emphasis is thus on 'God' and not on the 'Mother'. Evangelicals need have no scruples about accepting it as theologically sound, although they will wish to dissociate themselves from excessive veneration of Mary; they will often prefer 'God-bearer' as a more precise translation.